Macmillan CXC St

Jean R

WIDE SARGASSO SEA

Debbie Jacob

MACMILLAN
CARIBBEAN

Macmillan Education
Between Towns Road, Oxford, OX4 3PP
A division of Macmillan Publishers Limited
Companies and representatives throughout the world

www.macmillan-caribbean.com

ISBN-13: 978-1-4050-3092-2
ISBN-10: 1-4050-3092-5

Typeset by EXPO Holdings
Cover design by Clare Webber
Cover photograph by Pearl Freeman courtesy of The Jean Rhys Papers, The
University of Tulsa – McFarlin Library, Department of Special Collections.

Printed and bound in Thailand

2010 2009 2008 2007 2006
10 9 8 7 6 5 4 3 2 1

Contents

Introducing Macmillan Study Companions

Reading requires the skills of a detective because a reader must constantly gather clues to make sense of the events in a story, novel or play. Readers also have to function like detectives in order to understand characters and their conflicts.

The study companion that you are about to read is designed to aid you in your literary investigations. It provides background information about the author, sample essays, vocabulary, analysis and study questions – all useful tools to guide you on your mission.

A study companion is not a substitute for reading literature. A good detective always analyses original information and builds a case from a slew of first-hand witnesses. He uses a variety of sources and never relies on other people's opinions alone.

I am sure you will find the process of investigation challenging and rewarding. The world of literature is every bit as exciting as the real world we live in. Characters face the same situations and the same conflicts that challenge us in our everyday lives. Understanding those characters and their conflicts is the job of every reader.

Part I Analysing Literature

Comparing Two Writers – Two Biographies and a Sample Essay

The fictional character Antoinette Rochester offers a rare opportunity in literature to compare two different writers' versions of the same character. Undoubtedly these different interpretations came from the writers' own unique experiences and the ways that their vastly different cultures coloured their viewpoint of the world.

Below, you will find three separate essays. The first essay is a biography of Charlotte Brontë, author of *Jane Eyre*, and the second essay is a biography of Jean Rhys, author of *Wide Sargasso Sea*. The third essay compares information from both biographies.

Charlotte Brontë – A Lonely Childhood Spent in Fantasy

The cold, bleak setting of Thornton, Yorkshire, in England was much more than a backdrop for writer Charlotte Brontë's life. Born on April 21, 1816, the woman who would become immortalised through her famous classic *Jane Eyre* lived what could only be described as a lonely life.

Her mother, Maria Brontë, died when Charlotte was barely a year old and her father, Patrick, who was curate for life at the moorland parish of Haworth, Yorkshire, could hardly handle raising five daughters and a son. Left to the care of their aunt, Elizabeth Branwell, the children were sent to a religious boarding school. There the eldest daughters, Maria and Elizabeth, died in 1825 from tuberculosis.

The remaining children were then raised at home, where they populated their lonely world with make-believe characters from fictional countries. They indulged in Gothic fiction and staged their own plays.

Charlotte managed to spend a year studying at Miss Wooler's school in Roe Head. She became a teacher there from 1835 to

1838 and later went to work as a governess. Emily and Charlotte then studied languages at a boarding school in Brussels in 1842. Charlotte developed a crush on an instructor, M. Heger, who was a married man. She never pursued the relationship, but it undoubtedly fed her imagination when she came to write *Jane Eyre*. Later in 1842 Brontë's aunt died, and the sisters returned home. Charlotte afterwards managed to return to Brussels and teach.

In 1847 *Jane Eyre* was published under the pseudonym Currer Bell. Sister Anne had already published *Agnes Grey*, and Emily had already published *Wuthering Heights*. *Jane Eyre* was a hit with both the critics and the public, and it allowed Charlotte to settle down to additional writing. She married her father's curate, Arthur Bell Nicholls, in 1854. At last, her lonely existence had ended. But her marriage was short-lived: Charlotte died the following year on March 31, 1855.

Her novel *Jane Eyre* lived on. It is still one of the most popular classics.

Jean Rhys – A Restless Life

She made Europe her home and she wrote about her native Dominica with a touch of nostalgia, but Jean Rhys never truly felt a part of any country or culture. She was born Ella Gwendoline Rees Williams in Roseau, Dominica, in the West Indies. Her father was a Welsh doctor and her mother was a third-generation Dominican Creole of Scottish ancestry. Slavery had ended in Dominica in 1834, but the population, predominantly of African descent, never seemed to forget the social injustice. As a white Creole woman, Rhys always felt on the periphery of Dominican society.

For most of her childhood Jean Rhys lost herself in literature and dreamed of visiting far-away places. She attended a convent school in Roseau, until, when she was seventeen, her father sent her to live with an aunt in England. She briefly attended the Perse School, Cambridge (1907–8), and the Royal Academy of Dramatic Art in London (1909).

Her education came to a screeching halt when her father died. Rhys then worked as a chorus girl for a touring musical company, and she ghost-wrote a book about furniture. She became involved with older men and received a small allowance from a former lover. During World War I Rhys was a volunteer worker in a soldiers' canteen, and in 1918 she worked in a pension office.

In 1919 Rhys travelled to Holland and married the French-Dutch journalist and songwriter Jean Lenglet. She lived with him from 1920 to 1922 in Vienna and Budapest, then in Paris, and after 1927 mainly in England. They had two children, a son who died in infancy and a daughter.

Her passion for writing grew when she met the writer Ford Madox Ford, while she was in Paris, and he encouraged her to write. She must have welcomed the attention – by that time her husband was in prison for some illegal financial transactions. Rhys scraped together a living for herself and her daughter and became romantically involved with Ford Madox Ford. Their break-up was a bitter one. Rhys and her husband were eventually divorced.

In 1927 she published her first collection of stories, *The Left Bank and Other Stories*, under her pen name, Jean Rhys. The stories, like all her literature yet to be published, were highly autobiographical. Rhys's first novel, *Quartet* (1928), explored the sexual exploitation of the innocent; *After Leaving Mr Mackenzie* (1931) was yet another sad story about love, poverty and insecurity. Rhys continued her theme of women as victims in *Voyage in the Dark* (1934). In *Good Morning, Midnight* (1939) she describes an ageing woman, Sasha Jensen, coming to grips with life.

Rhys dropped out of the public eye from 1939 to 1957. She had moved to Devon, England, in 1939 and lived there in virtual seclusion. Her second husband, Leslie Tilden Smith, whom she married in 1934, died in 1945. Two years later she married his cousin Max Hamer, who had served a prison term and spent much of their marriage in gaol. He died in 1966.

Rumours began to surface that Rhys herself had died and it was not until those rumours were announced as news, on a BBC programme honouring her work, that Rhys resurfaced. She continued a pattern of heavy drinking, and resumed her writing with encouragement from Francis Wyndham. She remained secluded in her humble Devon cottage at Cheriton Fitzpaine.

Jean Rhys made a stunning literary comeback in 1966 when *Wide Sargasso Sea* was published. The story of the first Mrs Rochester met with both critical and public acclaim. She received many accolades, including the Royal Society of Literature award. On receipt of the W.H. Smith award in 1966, she made her hauntingly famous response, 'It has come too late.'

Jean Rhys died on May 14, 1979, in Exeter. At the time of her death, she was working on her autobiography, which was published posthumously as *Smile Please*. In the end her life seemed to be a constant search for love and acceptance.

Two Different Worlds Joined by the Same Character

Charlotte Brontë and Jean Rhys came from two vastly different worlds, but the distinctly different writers had more in common than the character of Antoinette Rochester, who was created by Brontë.

As girls, both writers possessed a passion for literature. Both dreamed of being writers, and education was important to them. Life was not easy for either Brontë or Rhys. For Brontë, the bitterly cold English landscape and lung problems that plagued her family were obstacles to overcome. For Rhys, the major battle was to feel safe and wanted, in a culture that rejected her because of her skin colour.

Both women suffered through the death of a parent while they were children. Brontë's mother died when she was barely a year old; Rhys's father died when she was seventeen. Their lives were changed forever after that parent had died. Both girls ended up living with an aunt.

While neither received very much education, both girls benefited from some travelling. This opened them up to new experiences and provided material for their books. Both women wrote about their experiences with men, but Brontë's were restricted to fantasy while Rhys plunged into what many would have considered the seedy side of life.

Brontë seemed to be absorbed with her work and did not marry until the end of her life, while Rhys's desire for love and relationships seemed to equal her passion for writing. She was married three times.

For all their differences, Brontë and Rhys are bound together for ever through their portrayal of Antoinette Rochester. Brontë created Antoinette, but Rhys provided her background. Together, the two writers achieved the pinnacle of success: they both wrote a classic work that has stood the test of time.

Jean Rhys's Letters – A Clue to the Past

Jean Rhys was always aware that *Wide Sargasso Sea* was an important novel. This is evident in a collection of her letters, *Jean Rhys: Letters 1931–1966*, edited by Francis Wyndham and Diana Melly in 1984. In a letter dated October 1945, Rhys referred to an early version of *Wide Sargasso Sea* that was half-finished: '[it is] the one book I've written that's much use', she wrote (p. 39).

Rhys agonised over the book that would become her signature piece for quite some time. She was thinking about calling it 'The First Mrs Rochester', 'with profound apologies to Charlotte Brontë and a deep curtsy too', she wrote in 1949 (*Letters*, p. 50). Rhys's admiration for Brontë's work, particularly her character of Antoinette Rochester, is evident in another letter, written in 1959. 'I did not mean to be impertinent about Charlotte Brontë', she wrote. 'I admire her greatly' (*Letters*, p. 175).

It was some time later that Rhys settled on the title of her work in progress as *Wide Sargasso Sea*. She noted that no one seemed to know what she was referring to, or realise that the Sargasso Sea really existed, when she told them the title (*Letters*, p. 154).

Although at times she doubted her ability to do justice to Antoinette Rochester's story, the need to tell it propelled Rhys forward. She talked about feeling quite shocked, as well as annoyed, when she first read about Antoinette Rochester (*Letters*, p. 297). 'It's quite true that I've brooded over *Jane Eyre* for years', she confided in Francis Wyndham in a letter dated 1964 (*Letters*, p. 262). 'The Brontë sisters had of course a touch of genius, especially Emily. So reading *Jane Eyre*, one's swept along regardless. But I, reading it later, and often, was vexed at her portrait of the "paper tiger" lunatic, the all wrong Creole scenes, and above all the real cruelty of Mr Rochester.'

Rhys wanted a character that was 'plausible with a past' (*Letters*, p. 156). She set out to create a feeling of warmth for Antoinette, both physically and emotionally. Antoinette searches for warmth in a physical sense while she is confined in England, and she spends her entire marriage struggling for emotional warmth.

For Rhys, there was a reason for Antoinette's bizarre behaviour and she would not allow it to be passed off as unexplainable madness. The reason Antoinette Rochester tries to set everything on fire is because she is cold. She sets fires, Rhys explained in one letter, to feel warm, physically and emotionally speaking.

Teeming with ideas, Rhys cautiously moved forward in her quest to tell the first Mrs Rochester's story. Whatever her battles, Rhys emerged sure of her quest. 'Take a look at *Jane Eyre*', she wrote in 1958. 'That unfortunate death of a Creole! I'm fighting mad to write her story' (*Letters*, p. 157).

Understanding the Background to *Wide Sargasso Sea*

Dominican writer Jean Rhys felt that the first Mrs Rochester received unjust treatment in Charlotte Brontë's novel *Jane Eyre*, so she set out to tell Antoinette's story in her own novel, entitled *Wide Sargasso Sea*. In order to understand Rhys's novel, we must investigate information provided in *Jane Eyre*. To judge Antoinette Rochester from the information in *Wide Sargasso Sea* alone would be a great injustice. Good investigations leave no stones unturned. *Jane Eyre* provides us with the opportunity to gather clues about Mr Rochester, to determine if the stories he tells Jane are correct. This information also helps to provide an understanding of Jane so that we can compare the two wives. Comparisons can offer useful clues about a character in a literary analysis. By understanding what kind of person Jane is, and why Mr Rochester is attracted to her, we can develop a picture that shows why he rejected Antoinette.

Antoinette Rochester Finds Her Place in Literature

Left to British writer Charlotte Brontë, the first Mrs Rochester would have been nothing more than a troublesome madwoman locked away in the tower for her own good. The world would have barely recognised the beauty and heartache of that free-spirited, Caribbean woman who became a prisoner in her husband's house.

Caribbean writer Jean Rhys set about the monumental task of telling the first Mrs Rochester's story by writing a prequel to *Jane Eyre*. The prequel allows readers to meet the first Mrs Rochester and understand her wretched life, and it gives us a rare opportunity to judge the actions of Mr Rochester. In *Jane Eyre*, readers must accept his version of the story about how Antoinette Rochester went mad and was locked away in the tower at Thornfield.

Wide Sargasso Sea allows Antoinette to tell her own story. It is arguably the most important and best-known piece of literature to emerge from the Caribbean, not because it gives Antoinette a voice, but because it allows Antoinette to represent women from third-world countries whose voices and opinions might otherwise have been lost. It is certainly one of the most used and best-loved books by a Caribbean writer.

Brontë may have haphazardly decided to make Antoinette a Caribbean woman. If she did, she never counted on her having the rights of an English woman to present her story as Jane Eyre did. Even in Victorian England, an English woman had more rights than a Caribbean woman. It is unlikely that an English woman could have been locked away in a tower and forgotten in history. In any case, Brontë could not have dreamed that Antoinette Rochester would have an author to champion her cause and present her story.

Thanks to Jean Rhys, the first Mrs Rochester was not forgotten. Her story stands alongside Jane Eyre's, and students throughout the world examine both books in high schools and universities. Neither book outweighs the other for literary merit. In the end, thanks to a Caribbean writer, the first Mrs Rochester's story became as important as the second Mrs Rochester's story. Jean Rhys succeeded in giving the Caribbean an important voice in literature. She sent an important message to her readers: the Caribbean and Caribbean women will not be a footnote in history or a footnote in literature. We will be heard.

Jane Eyre – On the Trail of the Woman who would become the Second Mrs Rochester

There is no role more challenging for a literary detective than the one you are about to begin: investigating the death of the first Mrs Rochester in the novel *Jane Eyre*. According to the mysterious Mr Rochester, his first wife was a madwoman whom he locked away in a tower for her own safety.

There is little doubt that Antoinette Rochester was a madwoman. The question is, what drove her mad? Did Mr Rochester have anything to do with her state of mind? Did Mr Rochester get away with murder, so to speak? We know that he did not kill Antoinette Rochester, but did he create unbearable circumstances for her to live? Did Mr Rochester fool Jane with a sob story about his early marriage? Did Mr Rochester carry off one of the greatest cases of emotional deceit in literature?

These are all questions worth debating. After all, who would simply take Mr Rochester's word for his wife's demise? It is a case worthy of investigation.

Linking Two Books

Antoinette Rochester is a minor character in Charlotte Brontë's *Jane Eyre*, but she is certainly not insignificant. Antoinette sets a whole series of events in motion and she impacts on Jane's life even before Jane knows she exists. She is Mr Rochester's obligation, and the weight of that commitment initially prevents his relationship with Jane.

Although Antoinette Rochester has only a minor role in *Jane Eyre*, Jean Rhys saw her value and transformed her from a minor to a major character by writing *Wide Sargasso Sea*, a prequel to the English classic *Jane Eyre*.

Prequels are rare in literature. We are more familiar with sequels, in both books and movies. Sequels continue an earlier story.

A prequel tells the story of what happened before a particular story.

To truly understand Antoinette Rochester, we need to work backwards and gather clues from *Jane Eyre* and then from *Wide Sargasso Sea*. In both books Mr Rochester is a key character to examine. *Wide Sargasso Sea*, however, is the only book that gives Antoinette a voice.

In *Jane Eyre*, Mr Rochester presents himself as the victim of a love gone bad, namely because his wife was mad. Antoinette Rochester is little more than an obstacle that stands in the way of Mr Rochester's and Jane's happiness.

Wide Sargasso Sea, on the other hand, tells of a relationship doomed because of the cultural differences and the peculiar set of obstacles that prevent happiness between Mr Rochester and Antoinette.

The story of Antoinette Rochester's love and madness is more than a personal story. It is a glimpse of what happens when two people from vastly different circumstances and two opposing cultures collide.

It is a story for our time.

Jane Eyre – Literature's First Feminist?

Jane Eyre is a bold, sometimes brazen young lady, who is determined to find a place for herself in the world in spite of her dire personal circumstances. Orphaned as a child, she goes to live with her maternal uncle, who also dies and leaves her with a cruel, uncaring aunt and cousins.

There at Gateshead Hall with her aunt, Mrs Reed, and her cousins, Jane fights against the physical and mental abuse she receives in the house. For that she is deemed ungrateful by her aunt. Constantly reminded of her abject poverty and the debt that she owes her mother's family, Jane holds on to her own sense of self-worth with admirable tenacity. She knows that her mother's decision to marry a poor clergyman resulted in her mother being disinherited, but Jane loved her parents and seems to gather strength from their idealistic notions of love.

Even as a child, Jane refuses to cower when people try to break her spirit. This audacity causes her cruel aunt to place her in Lowood, a strict school for destitute children. Lowood exposes Jane to all the social misfortunes of the day. Wracked by disease and an educational system determined to break children's spirits, Lowood offers nothing to its students – not even a decent meal. Still, Jane manages to survive. She even tries to offer comfort and encouragement to a sickly child, Helen.

Jane's optimism and determination are admirable qualities that propel her from one stage in life to the next. Because Jane is the heroine of her own story, we often initially assume certain negative feelings about the first Mrs Rochester by our unconscious comparison of the two women.

Unlike Jane, the first Mrs Rochester is weak both mentally and physically – she is a burden and someone to pity. Antoinette cannot deal with life; her madness appears to be a sign of weakness.

Jane is the antithesis of Antoinette. She is scrappy, bold, and outspoken. Jane is, quite likely, literature's first feminist. She rises above the injustices in her life – a cruel aunt, a harsh school, and a cold suitor – and creates her own place in this world. She never allows herself to be a victim. Jane refuses to be conquered by any emotion – even love. She pursues life with determination, and is in control of her life every step of the way. She is fiercely independent and she works to earn a living, shaping her own destiny at a time when women had very few rights.

Jane's independence and power can best be shown by the relationship she creates between the reader and Mr Rochester. We accept Mr Rochester, even though he is not a particularly kind or pleasant man, because he is Jane's choice, and we accept his explanation of his burdened life because Jane accepts it. This is extraordinary, considering Mr Rochester's negative personality. Jane Eyre's qualities – her optimism, independence, loyalty and love – make her a beloved character in literature.

Jane Eyre Meets Mr Rochester

After Jane Eyre leaves Lowood she places an advertisement in the newspaper for a job. Much to her surprise she receives a reply: 'J.E.

is requested to send references, name, address, and all particulars to the direction:—' writes Mrs Fairfax of Thornfield (*Jane Eyre*, p. 122).

With school behind her and her favourite teacher, Miss Temple, married and gone, Jane, who is only eighteen, travels to her new job as governess and teacher to Miss Adele Varens, Mr Rochester's ward. She learns that Adele is the daughter of a French opera singer with whom Rochester once had a 'grande passion' (p. 208). When the girl's mother abandoned her, Rochester brought her from France to Thornfield.

How Mr Rochester Acquired Thornfield

Mr Rochester took possession of Thornfield nine years before Jane met him. His father, who was said to be fond of money, did not want to divide his property because he felt it would diminish the value. His brother, Rowland, was given the property. Then Rowland died and the property was willed to Edward (Mr Rochester). Mrs Fairfax's story about how Rowland inherited his father's land is sketchy. All she knows is that the deal was not quite fair to her master, Mr Rochester.

Mrs Fairfax says that Rochester visits Thornfield irregularly and this upsets Adele, who came to live there at Mr Rochester's invitation. '[He] was kind to me and gave me pretty dresses and toys: but you see he has not kept his word, for he has brought me to England, and now he has gone back again himself, and I never see him', Adele laments (p. 151).

When Jane questions Mrs Fairfax about the elusive Mr Rochester, she is told that he is liked and respected by those who know him. 'His character is unimpeachable, I suppose', says Mrs Fairfax (p. 154). At the same time, she admits he is 'rather peculiar'.

Jane Meets Her Match

Jane first meets Mr Rochester when she is out walking in the grounds of Thornfield. Mr Rochester and his horse have slipped on a sheet of ice and Mr Rochester is injured. He refuses Jane's offer to get help and questions her without revealing who he is. Jane describes him as having a dark face, stern features, a heavy brow, and past youth, about thirty-five (p. 167). (He says he is twenty years older than Jane and therefore thirty-eight; p. 167.) He allows Jane to help him, and later Jane makes the connection that the man she met was Mr Rochester.

Mr Rochester is very formal with Jane at their first meeting. He invites her and Adele to tea, but he behaves rudely when Jane is introduced. Jane notices his injured foot propped up on a pillow and realises the connection to the man she helped. Although Mr Rochester questions her about her background and early life, he does not have any real conversation with her. He appears to be quite cold and callous. In their second meeting, Mr Rochester challenges Jane: 'You examine me, Miss Eyre ... Do you think me handsome?' (p. 194). Jane attributes his rude statements about her to his drinking, and he tells Jane that he is not as good as he would like to be.

'You intimated that to have a sullied memory was a perpetual bane', he says (p. 203). Jane realises that he is a troubled man. She grows fonder of Mr Rochester, but feels that he will probably marry Blanche Ingram, who lives on a neighbouring estate.

Mr Rochester Entertains

Mr Rochester comes and goes from Thornfield without any warning. One day after he returns, guests including Blanche and her sister Mary arrive for a visit. They ask Mr Rochester about Adele.

'Mr Rochester, I thought you were not fond of children?' Blanche asks (p. 261).

'Nor am I', he says.

'Then, what induced you to take charge of such a little doll as that?' Blanche asks. (She points to Adele.) 'Where did you pick her up?'

'I did not pick her up; she was left on my hands', Mr Rochester says.

'You should have sent her to school.'

'I could not afford it: schools are so dear.'

Mr Rochester's behaviour is startling, to say the least. He acts as though Adele is a burden, but he is the one who brought her to Thornfield. Besides that, he pays no attention to Jane until she leaves the room, apparently appalled at his behaviour. Mr Rochester follows Jane and asks her what she has been doing since he left. He says she looks pale and seems depressed. It appears that Mr Rochester is trying to make up for his cross behaviour, but on another evening, when the guests decide to play charades, and Mr Rochester invites Jane to play, Mary Ingram says, 'No, she looks too stupid for any game of the sort.' Mr Rochester does not say anything to defend Jane.

The Puzzling Mrs Rochester

Jane hears Antoinette before she ever sees her. As Jane makes her way through a long passage she hears laughter coming from the third storey, from behind 'small black doors all shut, like a corridor in some Bluebeard's castle'. Jane describes the laugh as 'curious ... distinct, formal, mirthless ... low'. 'It passed off in a clamorous peal that seemed to wake an echo in every lonely chamber ... the laugh was as tragic, as preternatural a laugh as any I ever heard ...' (p. 157).

Mrs Fairfax says the laughter is coming from a servant, Grace Poole, but Jane is suspicious because of a strange conversation that follows between Mrs Fairfax and Grace Poole when Grace comes out of a room: 'Too much noise, Grace,' said Mrs Fairfax. 'Remember directions!'

The second time Jane hears Antoinette's laughter, she describes it as 'demoniac' (p. 219). Jane sees footsteps going up the stairs to the third floor and she notices a fire in Mr Rochester's room. She saves his life. Mr Rochester calls on Jane's help again when Antoinette attacks Mr Mason and bites him. Jane still thinks Grace Poole is causing the problems and she cannot figure out why Mr Rochester puts up with her.

The Strange Arrival of an Unwelcome Guest

One night a stranger, who appears to know Mr Rochester well, arrives at Thornfield. Mr Mason, from Kingston, reveals much information about Mr Rochester. He says that Mr Rochester could not take the heat, hurricanes and rainy seasons of the tropics when he lived there.

A Gypsy Fortune Teller Stirs Up Controversy

Jane gladly goes to the fortune teller, when she is summoned by the mysterious Gypsy who arrives at Thornfield. The fortune teller says Jane is cold, sick, and silly, and she listens to the fortune teller's explanation. But the fortune teller turns out to be Rochester in disguise. He has upset a lot of people with his fortunes, but no one is as upset as he is when he learns that Mr Mason has arrived at Thornfield. That news makes Mr Rochester feel faint. Mr Mason leaves Thornfield in a rush, after he visits Antoinette and she bites him.

The Odd Proposal and Embarrassing Wedding

Mr Rochester pretends he is going to marry Miss Ingram when Jane returns from a visit to her dying aunt. Jane becomes upset and makes plans to leave Thornfield. Mr Rochester then springs his proposal on Jane. When Jane asks Mr Rochester how Miss Ingram will take the news, he answers: 'Her feelings are concentrated in one – pride; and that needs humbling. Were you jealous, Jane?' he asks (p. 392).

Mrs Fairfax does not appear happy about the upcoming wedding. She warns Jane: 'you are so young, and so little acquainted with men. I wished to put you on your guard. It is an old saying that "all is not gold that glitters"; and in this case I do fear there will be something found to be different to what either you or I expect.' But Jane's love propels her forward. She does not need Mr Rochester: when she went to visit her aunt, she collected a letter from an uncle, John Eyre, who wanted to adopt her – so she knows she has a home.

Mr Rochester asks Jane to give him her confidence, but Jane is confused by a premonition she had of Thornfield burning to the ground and a visit by a woman who is not Mrs Poole. Mr Rochester asks Jane to forget her vision and concentrate on her love, but Jane cannot forget the woman, whom she says looked like a vampire, looking at her wedding dress. Mr Rochester dismisses her fears and the two head for their wedding the next morning.

The wedding ceremony is interrupted by a solicitor named Mr Briggs who says that Mr Rochester is married. Mr Rochester responds: 'And you would thrust on me a wife?' (p. 434).

'I would remind you of your lady's existence, sir, which the law recognises, if you do not', the solicitor says.

Mr Rochester still pretends he does not know what is going on. 'Favour me with an account of her — with her name, her parentage, her place of abode.'

Mr Briggs obliges and Jane learns of Mr Rochester's marriage to Antoinette Mason, daughter of Jonas Mason, merchant, and Annette, his wife, a Creole, in Spanish Town, Jamaica. The letter is signed by Richard Mason, Antoinette's brother, who made an unannounced visit to Thornfield earlier.

Mr Rochester finally acknowledges his wife and carries everyone to the house to see her. He tells everyone that Antoinette is mad and that she comes from three generations of idiots and maniacs. Her history was kept secret from him, he insists, until after he was married. Jane retreats to her room. When she comes out, Mr Rochester tells her that he never meant to wound her. Jane decides to leave Thornfield. Mr Rochester says he too will leave. He will send Adele to school and pay Mrs Poole to stay on. Jane will not agree to be Rochester's mistress.

How Mr Rochester Married Antoinette

Before Jane leaves, Mr Rochester tells her the story of his marriage. He says his father, unable to bear the thought of dividing his beloved property, decided to leave his estate to the elder son, Rowland. He arranged for Mr Rochester to marry a wealthy woman. Mr Mason, a West Indian planter and merchant, was an old acquaintance of Mr Rochester's family. Mr Mason agreed that he would give a dowry of £30,000, a sufficient sum for Mr Rochester's father.

When Mr Rochester left college he was sent to Jamaica; he says he was told nothing about the money. He was told only of Antoinette's beauty and popularity. Mr Rochester says she was beautiful, but he knew little of her personality because he was seldom able to see her alone. 'She flattered me, and lavishly displayed for my pleasure her charms and accomplishments. All the men in her circle seemed to admire her and envy me. I was dazzled, stimulated: my senses were excited; and being ignorant, raw and inexperienced, I thought I loved her ... A marriage was achieved almost before I knew where I was ... I did not even know her' (p. 457).

He had never seen the bride's mother, but he understood that she was dead. He only found out later that she was in an insane asylum. Mr Rochester claims that his father and brother knew all this information and did not disclose it. Mr Rochester says he soon learned that he would never have a peaceful household because no servant would put up with his wife's violent and unrealistic temper. In the meantime his father and brother died.

One night, awakened by Antoinette's screams, Mr Rochester says, he decided to return to England. He brought her and locked her up at Thornfield. Then, he began to wander around Europe. After he completes his story, Mr Rochester asks Jane to stay with him, but Jane refuses. She leaves, becomes a teacher, inherits her uncle John's property and becomes rich.

Jane hears one day of the fire at Thornfield. A neighbour tells her that Antoinette started the fire and when Mr Rochester tried to save her, she jumped out of the third-floor window. Jane learns that Mr Rochester is blind. She volunteers to stay with him and nurse him back to health. He asks her to marry him. After they marry, Mr Rochester regains his eyesight.

Wide Sargasso Sea Vocabulary

abominable – detestable, loathsome
bane – cause of ruin or trouble, curse
blandishment – adulation, flattery
capricious – careless, irresponsible
commodious – roomy
debased – desecrated, defiled, belittled
disconcert – disturb the composure of, fluster
disdainful – vain, arrogant, cavalier

impeccable – exquisite, errorless, immaculate
inexorable – inevitable, unavoidable, stubborn
obstinate – stubborn
perpetual – continuous, infinite
posthumous – after death
reproach – reprimand, condemn, disgrace
reprobate – evil, wicked, bad
rigmarole – lengthy or complicated procedure; rambling or meaningless talk or tale
sullied – tainted, dirty
vulnerable – weak, defenceless

Vocabulary Exercise

1. Although Antoinette is portrayed as a _____ woman, she displays moments of great strength when she attacks her brother Richard Mason.
2. Mr Rochester's _____ relationship with Adele leaves Antoinette feeling angry and betrayed.
3. Jean Rhys never received the recognition that she deserved in her life. Many of her accolades and her autobiography, *Smile Please*, were published _____.
4. Antoinette found her mother's behaviour _____. Her mother changed moods quickly and Antoinette never knew how she would react to trouble.
5. Mr Rochester finds Christophene's behaviour _____ because she reacts to his threats in a carefree manner.
6. Daniel Cosway tries to _____ Antoinette's reputation by writing letters that expose her family history.
7. Christophene considers Antoinette to be an _____ person because Antoinette never listens to advice.
8. Antoinette feels that Mr Rochester is treating her unfairly, but Mr Rochester considers her family's lies and deceit to be the _____ of their marriage.
9. Mr Rochester seems to want an _____ bride. He leaves no room for mistakes or error.
10. Christophene thinks that Mr Rochester is an _____ man because he shows no mercy for Antoinette.

Part II Examining the Elements of Literature

Meet the Characters of *Wide Sargasso Sea*

1. Annette Cosway Mason – Antoinette's mother, a sensitive person, who never feels that she fits into Jamaican culture. She is from Martinique and she is described as being beautiful. Unable to cope with the prejudice that surrounds her, Annette slowly goes mad.

2. Antoinette – the beautiful Creole girl who becomes the first Mrs Rochester, the heroine of the story. Like her mother, Antoinette is sensitive and suspicious of those around her.

3. Pierre Cosway – Antoinette's younger brother, who has medical problems: one of the most tragic figures of the story. He cannot speak or walk properly. Pierre dies shortly after the fire at Coulibri Estate.

4. Aunt Cora – Antoinette's kind aunt, who takes the family in when their estate is burned; a pillar of strength for the family. She is a strong woman who encourages Antoinette not to give people the benefit of seeing her lose her sense of control. Mr Mason does not like her or approve of her because she is a former slave owner and somehow escaped the problems that other former slaver owners suffered, namely ridicule and prejudice.

5. Mr Mason – a kind and optimistic man who marries Annette and, for a time, rescues her from her insanity, is strong, determined, ambitious, and organised. These qualities help him to bring back his wife's estate, which is in total disarray when Mr Mason marries Annette. Mr Mason is kind to Antoinette and he seems to want to do what is best for her. Ironically, his kindness and optimism create a wedge between himself and his wife. He does not feel threatened by the non-white population and does not believe his wife, who seems to sense danger from the blacks on the island. Mr Mason knows Mr Rochester's father. Together they put the plan in motion to have Antoinette and Mr Rochester marry.

6. Richard Mason – said to be Antoinette's brother in *Jane Eyre*, but in *Wide Sargasso Sea* he is presented as Antoinette's stepbrother. He arranges Antoinette's marriage to Mr Rochester.

7. Christophene – a mysterious woman from Martinique, who is feared by the neighbours of Coulibri because she is said to practise obeah. Although she is distant and crass, she is a loyal servant of the Cosways.

8. Sandi Cosway – Alexander Cosway's son, who has a brief but important relationship with Antoinette. At one time, Antoinette thinks of Sandi as a cousin, but she knows that Mr Mason would not approve of her thinking of Sandi as family. Antoinette is fond of Sandi because he is kind to her when she goes to convent school and the other children tease her. Sandi represents the thousands of mixed-race inhabitants of the island.

9. Daniel Cosway – the illegitimate son of Antoinette's father and half-brother of Alexander Cosway; a selfish troublemaker who wrecks Antoinette's life.

10. Mr Rochester – an English gentleman who ends up marrying the Creole girl, Antoinette, because of an arrangement his father made with the Mason family.

11. Grace Poole – the woman who is hired to take care of Antoinette when Mr Rochester takes her to England. She is a strange, mysterious character.

Summary of *Wide Sargasso Sea*

Part One

Antoinette begins to narrate her own story in *Wide Sargasso Sea* with recollections of how her family felt ostracised by the rest of Jamaican society. As her mother's feelings of persecution increase, Antoinette's family becomes more isolated. Victimised by cruel acts, such as the poisoning of her mother's horse, the family withdraws more and more from Jamaican society. Antoinette's mother, who is a widow, retreats into her own private world. Antoinette becomes aware of social injustice, and how beauty causes jealousy.

As her mother becomes increasingly detached from her, Antoinette suffers alone. It is difficult for her to feel close to the servant Christophene, because Christophene pushes Antoinette away emotionally. Antoinette's mother is slipping away mentally and any hope of saving her seems to vanish with the doctor's report about Antoinette's younger brother, who cannot walk or talk properly.

Antoinette's mother manages to rally, and she regains some of her gaiety with the appearance of new neighbours, relatives of Mr Luttrell, who committed suicide. Annette marries Mr Jonas Mason in Spanish Town. He revamps Coulibri Estate but, within a year, Antoinette's mother becomes agitated and wants to leave. Her concerns about safety resurface and Mr Mason does not understand her fear. Even Antoinette feels that life was somewhat better before Mr Mason came, because her family was not so hated when they were poor. Antoinette's mother searches for ways to escape from Coulibri. Mr Mason tells his wife she is imagining problems.

One night 'a handful of drunk negroes', as Mr Mason puts it, set fire to the house. When the servant who is supposed to be with him disappears, Antoinette's brother nearly dies in the blaze. The family has to flee from the burning house. Someone stops to tell them that no one will be held accountable for the fire because those who set it will say it was an accident.

Antoinette's next recollection is six weeks later when her Aunt Cora tells her that she has been very ill. Antoinette's brother Pierre has died; her mother is said to be staying in the country. Antoinette asks Christophene to accompany her when she goes to visit her mother. Sadly, Annette is not able to respond to her daughter. Antoinette returns to Aunt Cora and attends convent school where the children tease her mercilessly about her race, her past, and her mother's insanity. They say that she is mad also. But Antoinette settles in school and considers it her refuge. She is not happy, but she can function even when she hears that her mother had died a year previously, and no one had bothered to inform her.

Part one ends with a visit from Jonas Mason. Antoinette is over seventeen, a grown woman by her own account. Mr Mason says that Aunt Cora is coming back from England and that Antoinette will live with him and Aunt Cora. He asks how she would like to live in England, saying that he wants her to be happy and that he has tried to arrange things. He says that he has invited English friends to stay.

Part Two

Some time has elapsed since Antoinette told the story of her childhood and now, in part two of *Wide Sargasso Sea*, Mr Rochester takes over as narrator. He, Antoinette, and a servant girl, Amelie, have travelled to the Windward Islands, to Antoinette's mother's remote mountain estate, Granbois, which seems to be in Dominica. Mr Rochester is agitated and unhappy, and Antoinette tries to cheer him up. She feels comfortable in the isolation, he does not.
Mr Rochester begins to watch his wife more critically. He says he was in Jamaica for just a month before he married her, and for three weeks he was ill with a fever.

Mr Rochester does not like the people he meets. He notes Amelie's expressions are full of 'delighted malice' and he finds Christophene frightening. He finds the isolation of Granbois unsettling, and his wife baffling, and remembers how, the night before the wedding, she had wanted to call it off. He recalls how Richard Mason, who is presented in *Jane Eyre* as Antoinette's brother and in *Wide Sargasso Sea* as her stepbrother, was irate when Antoinette made the suggestion to call off the wedding.
Mr Rochester admits that he was worried about the embarrassment that cancelling the wedding would cause. He begins to find fault with everything and everyone at Granbois. Antoinette becomes more and more afraid of losing the happiness that she does sometimes feel.

Whatever slim chance the marriage had is lost when Mr Rochester receives a letter from Daniel Cosway, who claims to be Antoinette's half-brother and illegitimate son of Antoinette's father. Daniel Cosway tells Mr Rochester that he has been fooled and that Antoinette is mad like her mother.

Antoinette becomes agitated when she learns that Christophene is planning to leave Granbois. She is increasingly upset about Amelie's disrespect and the fact that her husband does nothing about her rudeness. Mr Rochester watches everyone with suspicion because he feels that they all – including his own father – knew about the mental problems that run in Antoinette's family.

Sensing that Mr Rochester is slipping away from her, Antoinette asks for Christophene's advice about how to make him love her. Christophene suggests that Antoinette leave Mr Rochester and play coy, so that he will become interested in her again. Antoinette thinks about the proposition, but she is also thinking about the possibility of going to England. Mr Rochester has begun calling Antoinette by the name Bertha. This disturbs her and she tells him repeatedly, 'That is not my name.'

Mr Rochester realises that Amelie is delivering Daniel Cosway's disturbing letters. He asks her to stop, but curiosity gets the better of him and he goes to visit Daniel. Daniel tries to blackmail Mr Rochester. Disgusted, Mr Rochester leaves, and confronts Antoinette about her past. She tells him everything. Haunted by questions about his wife's family and former life, he writes to Mr Fraser, the Spanish Town magistrate. He asks questions about Christophene.

Rochester flirts with Amelie and has an affair with her. Antoinette is devastated and Christophene chastises Rochester for his callous behaviour. She accuses him of marrying Antoinette only for her money, and asks him to give back half the dowry and leave Antoinette in peace. Christophene says that they will go to Martinique, and travel, and that Antoinette will marry someone else. This enrages Rochester and he tells Christophene to leave. He threatens to put her out and reminds her that he now owns the estate. She leaves without saying goodbye to Antoinette, because she had given Antoinette something to make her sleep when she was distraught.

Mr Rochester decides that he will take Antoinette back to Spanish Town, where they will live in a spacious house. He vows that she will never return to this place that she loved. He watches all Antoinette's emotions – even her hate for what he has done – die, and he longs for the day when she is nothing more than a bad memory that he has locked away forever.

Part Three

Grace Poole tells the story of how she came to take care of Antoinette. Wary of taking care of someone who looked physically as well as mentally ill, Poole hesitated in taking the job but was lured by a generous salary.

Antoinette then narrates her own story again. Clearly she feels like a prisoner, and she realises that Grace Poole has been tempted by money. Antoinette has been told that she is in England, but she does not believe it. She has no recollection of the events that happen in *Jane Eyre*. She does not remember lighting the fire, attacking Richard, or approaching Jane. Cold and haunted by her past, particularly her relationship with Sandi, Antoinette struggles with her reality. She remembers how Mr Rochester used to call her Bertha. One night, while Grace Poole is sleeping, Antoinette takes the keys, opens the door, and takes a candle down the long passage. 'Now at last I know why I was brought here and what I have to do', says Antoinette (*Wide Sargasso Sea*, p. 124).

Investigating Place – The Geography of the Wide Sargasso Sea

The Sargasso Sea has baffled scientists and explorers since Christopher Columbus first wrote about it on his voyage to the West Indies. Columbus could not fathom that there actually was a sea in the middle of the ocean. When he first encountered the Sargasso Sea, he thought it was an indication that land was near. He got the surprise of his life.

The Sargasso Sea gets its name from sargassum, a Portuguese word for the dense seaweed that floats on top of the sea. Occupying that part of the Atlantic between 20° to 35° north latitude and 30° to 70° west longitude, the Sargasso Sea is nothing like the ocean that surrounds it.

Some of the strongest currents in the world circle the Sargasso Sea, which lies virtually motionless. It is a large trap for ships that inadvertently venture into its vast pools of stagnant seaweed.

The water itself under the seaweed is said to be clear. The Florida, Gulf Stream, Canary, North Equatorial, Antilles, and Caribbean currents interlock to separate this sea from the rest of the Atlantic. Anything that drifts onto any surrounding currents eventually ends up in the Sargasso Sea amidst its large mats of seaweed. Trapped by the tangle of seaweed, virtually nothing that enters the Sargasso Sea ever drifts away. The only noticeable movement in the Sargasso Sea is a slight rotation caused by the shifting currents during different seasons of the year (National Geographic). At one time, scientists thought the Sargasso Sea was a collection of seaweed floating out into the ocean. Now, they have changed their minds. They now think it is vegetation that has adapted and reproduced in the middle of the ocean.

Over the centuries there have been legends about ships and later even planes lost in the Bermuda Triangle, which is part of the Sargasso Sea. Sometimes sailors see the ships totally intact but with no one on board. One slave ship was spotted with nothing but skeletons on board.

The *Rosalie* sailed through this area in 1840 before later turning up derelict, as reported in the London *Times*. In 1881 the schooner *Ellen Austin* supposedly found a derelict schooner and, placing a prize crew aboard, sailed in tandem for port. Two days later the schooner was sighted sailing erratically. When it was boarded again, the ship was found to be once again deserted. There was no trace of the crew. The *James B. Chester* was found deserted in the Sargasso Sea in 1857, with chairs kicked over and a stale meal on the mess table. Modern derelicts have included the *Connemara IV*, found drifting 140 miles from Bermuda in 1955, plus a number of yachts and sailboats found in 1969 and 1982 (information gathered from the National Geographic website).

The Setting

Setting is the element of literature that is often taken for granted. Readers often do not stop to think how important setting is to a story, play or novel. Setting can put literature in context and always includes time and place. It is the showcase for characters and their conflicts, but it also helps to set the tone.

The use of multiple settings in a novel might seem disconcerting to some readers, but Jean Rhys's use of three settings in the relatively tiny book of Wide Sargasso Sea serves the purpose of creating that tangled web – like seaweed – that binds the characters together.

Part one of Wide Sargasso Sea takes place in Coulibri Estate, the home of Antoinette and her family, near Spanish Town, Jamaica, during the 1830s. It is set after the Emancipation Act of 1833. (Full emancipation occurred in 1838.)

Antoinette's honeymoon takes place on another family estate, Granbois, which seems to be in Dominica. This too is a remote place. It is a stark contrast to Thornfield, Mr Rochester's home in England, where part three of the book takes place.

The settings form a triangle that traps the characters, much like the Bermuda Triangle within the Sargasso Sea.

Spanish Town, Jamaica, in the 1830s

Spanish Town, also known as St Jago de la Vega, was once the capital city of Jamaica. Built on the west bank of the Rio Cobre, Spanish Town is located just thirteen miles from Kingston on the main road. According to the National Library of Jamaica, Spanish Town became the centre of Jamaican life and history from the time it was established. It was a vibrant commercial route that connected Jamaica, Spain and other Spanish territories. In spite of its commercial success, Spanish Town was not a particularly stable place. Systematic attacks on Jamaica by other European nations trying to dislodge the Spanish government demoralised the residents.

The British finally managed to take over on May 10, 1655, under an expedition led by Admiral William Penn and General Robert Venables. This marked the end of Spanish occupation in Jamaica. When the British conquered Jamaica they renamed the city Spanish Town.

The British did not find ruling Spanish Town an easy task. They found the city looted when they took it over, and they met fierce opposition from the Maroons, slaves who had escaped from the Spanish and were living in the mountains. The Maroons attacked the British, killing soldiers and burning British houses. The town gradually became the island's administrative centre. An earthquake that damaged Port Royal on June 7, 1692, thrust Spanish Town back into a position of power. The city played an important role for the British for nearly a hundred and eighty years.

Probing the Narrator

Jean Rhys agonised over one major problem in *Jane Eyre*: Charlotte Brontë's decision to stifle Antoinette Rochester's voice. Fascinated by Mr Rochester's first wife, a Creole girl from the Caribbean, Rhys took the bold decision to tell her story. Rhys knew that she could appear fair only by allowing Mr Rochester a voice in Antoinette's story, *Wide Sargasso Sea*. She was determined not to commit the same mistake as Brontë by writing a story that condemns a character without any defence for their behaviour.

Rhys's feelings are clearly voiced by Antoinette, when Mr Rochester confronts her with Daniel Cosway's bitter letter that accuses the family of grave deceptions. Antoinette replies: 'He tells lies about us and he is sure that you will believe him and not listen to the other side' (p. 82).

'Is there another side?' Rochester asks.

'There is always the other side, always', says Antoinette.

Rhys's desire to be fair results in an interesting narrative technique. *Wide Sargasso Sea* is divided into three parts. Antoinette narrates part one. Here, she provides the reader with her family's history. Part two is narrated by Mr Rochester, and Rhys gives Rochester a full eighty pages to make his case against his wife. This is twice the space that she affords Antoinette, who returns to narrate her own story in part three. Rhys employs another interesting technique by bringing Grace Poole into the picture at the beginning of part three, to tell how she came to take care of Antoinette.

The various narrators of *Wide Sargasso Sea* – Antoinette, Mr Rochester, Grace Poole – create a tangled web of information that develops the theme of the wide Sargasso Sea.

Investigating Rhetorical Devices – Establishing Tone

When it comes to establishing tone, authors have as many tricks up their sleeves as magicians. Those tricks are part of a well-structured plan to get readers to see what the author wants them to see.

Some authors use the illusion of figures of speech – metaphors, similes and personification – to get the reader to see a certain image. Others use vocabulary, punctuation and grammar to create a visual image of a character by the way he expresses himself. Rhys uses vivid imagery and clever turns of phrase to create a sombre, eerie tone in *Wide Sargasso Sea*. She juxtaposes images unexpectedly, to catch the reader off balance and create a sense of irony.

One such example occurs at the beginning of the novel with Mr Luttrell, a kind neighbour who seems to understand the restlessness of the former slaves. He explains their callous, threatening behaviour by saying that they are waiting for compensation from the British for the Emancipation Act. 'Some will wait for a long time', he says (p. 5). In the next paragraph, Rhys says Mr Luttrell was the first to grow tired of waiting: 'One calm evening he shot his dog, swam out to sea and was gone for always.' Antoinette learns that you cannot count on anyone: you cannot truly know anyone. This creates a feeling of insecurity, and the feeling of uneasiness contributes to the sombre tone.

Another example of juxtaposing images effectively occurs when Antoinette describes her home on Coulibri Estate as a 'garden ... large and beautiful as that garden in the Bible' (p. 6). The garden as something pure and Biblical quickly turns into an ominous place where everything has grown wild. Orchids begin looking like snakes and octopuses.

Rhys gets a lot of mileage out of contrasting images. Initial images of innocence and beauty turn ugly and horrible, creating a depressing feeling of loss. This occurs again when Antoinette and Mr Rochester spend their honeymoon in a tropical island paradise that conjures up images of blissful seclusion – until the reader is told that the isolated estate is near a place called Massacre.

The clever turns of phrase that Rhys often employs are Antoinette's best defence against Mr Rochester's accusations of deception. Although Mr Rochester insists that he has been deceived, Rhys adeptly shows how language can create misunderstandings that are not outright deceptions.

When Antoinette recovers from her fever after the fire, she enquires about her brother, Pierre.

'He died on the way down, the poor little boy', says Aunt Cora (p. 25).

'He died before that,' Antoinette thinks. That is, Pierre really had no life because of his illnesses.

There are many subtle turns of phrases that are quite revealing. At seventeen, with school nearly behind her, Antoinette is told by her stepbrother Richard that he wants her to be happy and secure: 'I've tried to arrange it', he says (p. 33). Of course the reader realises that happiness and security have to come from within; they are not feelings that can be arranged arbitrarily by someone else, even if the concern is genuine.

Mr Rochester rants and raves about being deceived throughout *Jane Eyre* and *Wide Sargasso Sea*, but Rhys's clever way of juxtaposing images and turns of phrase seem to suggest that Mr Rochester's carelessness as well as his misinterpretation of West Indian culture are at least partly responsible for his predicament.

The Role of Minor Characters

Minor characters often play the most interesting role in a novel because they can set in motion events that affect major characters. Sandi and Daniel Cosway, and Grace Poole, make brief appearances in *Wide Sargasso Sea*, but their presence adds to the intrigue of the novel and sets certain conflicts in motion.

Sandi Cosway, the son of Alexander Cosway, proves to be a good friend to Antoinette when she is having trouble with children teasing her at school, at the beginning of the novel. By the time Antoinette marries Mr Rochester, Sandi's name is being tossed about as Antoinette's lover.

This creates confusion for Mr Rochester, who is beginning to question everything about Antoinette's behaviour. It is also considered to be an embarrassment for the family because Sandi is racially mixed. In a racially charged novel, Antoinette's possible sexual liaison with Sandi creates a feeling of crossing unspeakable boundaries.

Daniel Cosway stirs up controversy and provides Mr Rochester with the evidence that he needs against his wife and her family, as doubts about their honesty begin to grow. At first Daniel Cosway sends letters to Mr Rochester; later he meets him in person and makes a case against the family. He accuses the Masons of being dishonest, prejudiced, and cruel. He also provides information about the family's history of madness and the untimely death of Annette, Antoinette's mother. Daniel Cosway makes only a small appearance in *Wide Sargasso Sea*, but he sets in motion the events that will unravel Antoinette's marriage.

Grace Poole makes a brief appearance in both *Jane Eyre* and *Wide Sargasso Sea*. She is an essential character because she agrees to take care of Antoinette when Mr Rochester brings his first wife to England. The character of Grace Poole helps to add to the mystery of *Jane Eyre* because Antoinette's strange actions and bizarre laughter are blamed on Poole. She also allows an avenue to open so that the plot can develop. Because Grace Poole has obviously taken the job for the money and not for any humanitarian reasons, it seems that she does not keep an adequate watch over Antoinette.

In *Wide Sargasso Sea*, Grace Poole's brief narration of how she came to take care of Antoinette serves as a transition between Antoinette's life in the West Indies and Antoinette's life in England. That brief narration also serves as a link between *Wide Sargasso Sea* and Charlotte Brontë's novel *Jane Eyre*.

It is clear to see that these three minor characters have a major role in *Wide Sargasso Sea*. They all set events in motion that help to move the plot forward.

Analysing Character – A Literary Detective's Greatest Challenge

If you know a character's thoughts, feelings and motivations for doing things, then you have a handle on your job as a literary detective. Knowing a character might seem like a daunting task unless you have a plan for investigating. Just keep in mind the five methods of characterisation.

Here are the five methods of characterisation:

1. How a character looks – his physical appearance.
2. How a character acts – how he displays his personality.
3. How a character talks – how he shows both emotion and upbringing. A character who speaks in slang and curses, for instance, creates a certain image.
4. What a character thinks – what is in a character's mind.
5. How other characters react towards him – do they respect or hate him, for example?

There are two types of characters:

1. Stock characters or static characters do not undergo any specific change in a story. They are often used as character foils. In other words, their presence brings out certain characteristics in the protagonist of the story.
2. Dynamic characters or round characters undergo major changes in a story. They are often the most interesting characters because of their personal growth.

Let's investigate the characters in *Wide Sargasso Sea* and categorise them as stock or dynamic characters. Below, find a list of the characters. Think about their actions and jot down how you would categorise them. Detailed analysis follows this list.

1. Annette Cosway Mason
2. Antoinette

3. Pierre Cosway
4. Aunt Cora
5. Mr Mason
6. Richard Mason
7. Christophene
8. Sandi Cosway
9. Daniel Cosway
10. Mr Rochester
11. Grace Poole

Be the Judge – Static or Dynamic Characters?

1. Annette Cosway Mason – always seems to be on the periphery of Jamaican society. Rhys tells us that Jamaican women envied her and ostracised her from the time she arrived from Martinique. She is always suspicious, cynical, and upset. Her uneasiness progresses into outright madness. Although she straddles the border between sanity and insanity for a time, there are no major changes in Annette Cosway Mason. She is best classified as a static character.

2. Antoinette – like her mother, Antoinette is sensitive and suspicious of those around her. She questions her life constantly. She begins the novel as a keenly observant, sensitive child who is lucid and hopeful at times. She has her doubts about marrying Mr Rochester, but she believes in love and tries to make him happy. Consumed by jealousy and self-doubt, she works herself into an emotional state. By the end of the novel she is stark raving mad. Antoinette undergoes some subtle changes, but they are arguably enough to categorise her as a dynamic character.

3. Pierre Cosway – Antoinette's younger brother has medical problems that never improve. He undergoes no changes whatsoever, so he is a static character.

4. Aunt Cora – Antoinette's kind, strong aunt is reliable. Even though she leaves the country for a while, she returns and the family can count on her. She is a pillar of strength and her

personality never changes in any measurable way. She is a static character.

5. Mr Mason – accepts his wife's insecurity as well as her fears. Plodding on, he turns her dilapidated estate, Coulibri, into a thriving place that is the envy of jealous neighbours. He never heeds his wife's warnings and when the estate is finally razed, Mr Mason gets his family out with little emotion. He undergoes no major changes in the novel, emotionally speaking, so he is a static character.

6. Richard Mason – arranges Antoinette's marriage to Mr Rochester with little passion. He shows no concern for her feelings at any time. He never budges from his cold, calculating ways and that makes him a static character.

7. Christophene – a strong woman who speaks her mind. There are rumours that she dabbles in obeah. This increases her sense of mystery and power. Christophene encourages Antoinette to be strong and stand up for herself. She never indulges in pity and she never lets down her guard. She is a static character who undergoes no major changes in the novel.

8. Sandi Cosway – Alexander Cosway's son is really only alluded to in the novel. He is not fully developed as a character so we cannot judge him. If we had to categorise him, he would be a static character because there are no references that suggest any changes in him.

9. Daniel Cosway, the illegitimate son of Antoinette's father and half-brother of Alexander Cosway, is a bitter man who vents his anger in letters designed to poison Mr Rochester's mind. He never shows an ounce of compassion. When he meets Mr Rochester face to face, he tries to blackmail him. Daniel Cosway is a static character.

10. Mr Rochester is a suspicious man who indulges in a lot of self-pity. Although he says he is trying to make his marriage to Antoinette work, he appears to be unemotional and uncaring. He blames the marriage on his illness and claims that he was duped into marrying Antoinette. His emotions for Antoinette do not undergo any major change. He seems to barely tolerate her from the time they are married. Mr Rochester is arguably a static character.

11. Grace Poole is a cold, heartless woman who serves as nothing more than Antoinette's guard. She never demonstrates compassion – or any other feeling, for that matter. She is a static character.

Folklore Characters: Jumbie and Soucriant

Rhys alludes to two folklore characters in *Wide Sargasso Sea*. They are jumbies, which are often thought of as spirits, and soucriant (often written as soucouyant). Soucouyant are West Indian versions of vampires. Alluding to these folklore characters helps to add a sense of superstition to the novel. Soucouyant and many other folklore characters in the English-speaking and French-speaking Caribbean originated in Maritinique among the slaves.

Theme

The theme is the essence of a story, novel or play. Good novels usually develop more than one theme.

Wide Sargasso Sea has many themes: it probes the meaning of family, love, culture, jealousy, and loyalty. We explore these themes in more detail in part three of this study companion, on writing essays.

Analysing Conflicts

Conflicts create the excitement in fiction. Without conflicts, a novel would be a dull succession of events. Characters would not have to make choices in the way we have to in our own lives. Readers often relate to a character because of that character's conflicts. If we can identify with these conflicts, we identify with the character.

The easiest and best way to examine conflicts is to list characters and think about their actions in the novel. Determine how to categorise the characters' conflicts. Are they internal conflicts or external conflicts?

Internal conflicts are those that happen within a character. Making a decision is an internal conflict. Should I sneak out of the house and risk being punished by my parents? That is an internal conflict. Although these conflicts can be silent, they still add a certain energy to a story because they make a character – and the reader as well – wrestle with moral issues.

External conflicts involve a visual interaction between the character and his or her environment or another culture. Man against nature stories are filled with external conflicts, where characters have to make decisions about survival. *Moby Dick* is filled with external conflicts between the sailors and the whale. Fist fights, sword fights, and gun battles also involve external conflicts.

Here are some examples of character and conflict analysis in *Wide Sargasso Sea.*

1. Annette Cosway Mason is plagued with conflicts, most of which are external. From the time she comes to Jamaica, she is in direct conflict with jealous neighbours who scorn her for her beauty as well as her colour. This raises an interesting conflict for Annette. The one certainty that she has in her life is her beauty, but she cannot acknowledge her own beauty without bringing down the wrath of others. It is ironic that Annette's only sense of self, her beauty, causes her so much pain and suffering.

    Annette is also in direct conflict with her neighbours because she has property and she once had wealth. She allows Coulibri Estate to become run down because she is emotionally, financially, and physically unable to take care of it, but allowing her property to deteriorate also offers some kind of superficial protection from envious eyes.

    Annette engages in a struggle to protect and save her family from the time angry Jamaicans poison her horse and burn down her estate. Her conflict always lies in how to do this. While her new husband, Mr Mason, chooses to ignore those who are jealous of them, Annette chooses to retreat from the battle.

    Although Annette seems to be struggling with her sanity, she does not perceive this to be an issue in her life: she feels that her paranoia is justified. Still, a reader is abundantly aware of Annette's internal struggle with her sanity. This becomes even clearer when she is confined to a home in the country after the fire.

2. Antoinette: at the beginning of *Wide Sargasso Sea*, Antoinette's struggle seems to be mainly internal. She is trying to survive her mother's erratic behaviour. At the same time, there is a conflict with the children who categorise her as a 'white cockroach'. At school she is teased mercilessly. Antoinette has to decide how to deal with these conflicts. To ignore them makes her feel weak; to give in to them makes her lose her sense of dignity. This is her constant battle.

   Later, Antoinette has to reconcile herself to the destruction of her home. This raises a difficult conflict for her because she has to decide whether or not to acknowledge her mother's past raving as being prophetic. This makes Antoinette question her own sanity. This is the basis of Antoinette's conflict for the rest of the book. She has to choose between expressing herself freely and being deemed mad.

3. Richard Mason is a cold, calculating character whose main conflict centres on his need to get rid of his stepsister, Antoinette. He has to decide whether or not he is going to lie to Mr Rochester and withhold information so that he can get his sister married, or be honest and truthful and probably ruin his chances to rid himself of Antoinette. Of course he chooses the former.

   The night before the wedding, Richard Mason must decide how to pull the wedding off, because Antoinette wants to cancel it. He has to decide whether he will allow her to have her way or suffer the embarrassment that will ensue. He plays his trump card by informing Mr Rochester. Clearly he knows that Mr Rochester will not suffer the embarrassment of a cancelled wedding. Richard Mason deals with his internal conflicts in a very clever way: he manipulates people to solve his problems.

4. Christophene's conflicts are among the most interesting in the book. She has to decide whether her loyalties lie with her employers, who are of a different race from her, or the Jamaicans who ostracise her for being from Martinique. Because the Jamaicans categorise her as an obeah woman, the decision is partly made for her. Christophene, it seems, does not want

to betray her own sense of cultural identity to please the Jamaicans.

Later in the novel, Christophene has to decide whether she is going to take Mr Rochester's insults and stand by Antoinette, or abandon Antoinette to his whims. She gives Antoinette some questionable advice: leave Mr Rochester and make him jealous.

Although most of Christophene's problems are cleverly disguised internal problems, she does have one major external conflict: a verbal fight with Mr Rochester, who dismisses her from her job.

5. Mr Rochester's main external conflict is his struggle to survive in a foreign culture that he neither understands nor likes. He also has to figure out how he will deal with an arranged marriage to a woman he does not know. His internal conflicts include the tug of war between complying with his father's wishes to marry Antoinette, and his desire to escape the wedding until Antoinette decides to back out. Then his main internal conflict becomes whether embarrassment is preferable to happiness.

Once he is married, Mr Rochester has to decide how to deal with his wife's erratic behaviour. His internal conflict becomes whether he should overlook it or deal with it. His main internal conflict in part two of *Wide Sargasso Sea* is whether to have an affair with Amelie. His indiscretion leads to a major external conflict with Antoinette.

Mr Rochester's decision to return to England hardly seems like a conflict for him. His main conflict here is whether or not he should fulfil his obligation to his family and Antoinette's family. He must decide either to abandon her or take her along.

It seems that he takes the latter route because he is incensed by Christophene's request to return half of Antoinette's dowry and set her free. Mr Rochester has no shortage of external or internal conflicts.

6. Grace Poole's internal conflict lies in her decision about whether or not to take the job of caring for Antoinette. While she realises that the offer is not a particularly enjoyable one, she does have the money to consider, since Mr Rochester is offering what

seems to be a lucrative salary. Any moral issues that Grace Poole battles are outweighed by the financial gains. She takes the job and her only conflict then becomes how to survive Antoinette's outbursts, which make for colourful external conflicts.

Irony

A writer uses a variety of tools to shape prose. One of the most effective tools is irony. We often think of irony as sarcasm or humour, but irony is really when the unexpected occurs.

There are three types of irony that are used in literature:

1. Dramatic irony occurs when the narrator provides information for the reader so that the reader knows what is going to happen before the characters do. The most well-known case of dramatic irony in literature is in *Romeo and Juliet*. From the opening chorus, we know that the star-crossed lovers are doomed to die. But Romeo and Juliet do not know that. They spend the entire play trying to find a way to be together.

   Wide Sargasso Sea is based on the same dramatic irony. We know the relationship between Antoinette and Mr Rochester is doomed before they ever get married because Rhys's novel is a prequel.

2. Verbal irony comes from puns or turns of phrase that gives certain words or sentences a double meaning. Sometimes it passes for sarcasm. There is verbal irony in part two of *Wide Sargasso Sea* when Mr Rochester finds out that Antoinette's family estate in the Windward Islands is located near a place called Massacre.

   One would not expect a couple to spend their honeymoon in Massacre. Mr Rochester assumes the name comes from an incident in which slaves were killed, but he is assured that slaves were not slaughtered there. Something must have happened, he is told, but no one can remember what.

   This too is ironic because one would expect people to remember the reason for such a sinister name. This discussion serves as a foreshadowing of the events to come. By the end of part two the reader can look back to the beginning and understand yet another irony: another massacre occurred. This time it was the symbolic massacre of love and trust, and the emotional massacre of Antoinette.

3. Situational irony comes from the circumstances surrounding something that happens. It can be comical or farcical and comes from exaggeration.

An example of situational irony occurs when Mr Rochester and Antoinette are on their honeymoon. Mr Rochester chooses to have an affair with Amelie, his wife's servant. This is certainly unexpected.

Mr Rochester's marriage also qualifies for situational irony. Rochester marries so that he will feel rich and secure, but instead he ends up emotionally bankrupt.

Wide Sargasso Sea Quiz

1. Why do the 'white' people in Wide Sargasso Sea not accept Annette Cosway?
2. What happens when Annette persuades the doctor from Spanish Town to examine her son, Pierre?
3. Why is Coulibri compared to 'that garden in the Bible'?
4. Why does no one outside the Cosway/Mason household accept Christophene?
5. What cruel description do the children give Antoinette? What do you suppose the description means?
6. What happened to Antoinette's father?
7. Why does Mr Mason marry Annette?
8. Why does Mr Mason not approve of Aunt Cora?
9. Describe Mr Mason.
10. What is the significance of the green parrot, Coco, trapped in the fire that was set at Coulibri Estate?
11. What is Aunt Cora's advice to Annette when they are leaving the burning estate at Coulibri, and why is that advice important?

12. What happens to Antoinette's mother after the fire at Coulibri?
13. Mr Rochester and Antoinette spend their honeymoon on another island outside Jamaica. When they arrive at the Granbois Estate, Mr Rochester asks the name of the village. He is told the name is Massacre. What is ironic about this?
14. Antoinette is troubled even before the disastrous marriage. What exactly is bothering Antoinette emotionally, and how is that problem compounded by the marriage?
15. Daniel Cosway writes an emotional letter to Mr Rochester. What are some of the emotions conveyed in that letter?
16. Why does Mr Rochester call Antoinette Bertha?
17. Why did Christophene have to leave Spanish Town?
18. Why does Mr Rochester take Antoinette to England with him?
19. In part three Antoinette says she does not believe that she is in England. Why do you think that Antoinette doubts where she is?
20. What is the significance of the end of the book when Antoinette walks through the dark passage?

Part III Analysing and Writing Essays

Examining an Essay: An Effective Rubric for Writing

There are many ways to write an essay and examine the content of a piece of literature. Essentially, you can think of your essay in three parts. Here is the basic structure of an essay.

Beginning

The beginning should be clear, concise, and creative. A good beginning should focus the reader's attention. Creativity comes from establishing an unusual angle that few people would consider. It also comes from creating interesting visual links for the reader.

Support

Good support clearly demonstrates that there is important evidence for the points you are making in your beginning. Support should also be clear and concise. Each paragraph should be like a mini-essay, with a topic sentence serving as something comparable to the thesis statement, at least three sentences that support the topic sentence, and a conclusion for the paragraph.

Conclusion

A conclusion should remind the reader what the essay was about. It should not merely be a rewrite of the beginning of the essay. It should bring all the points together into a logical conclusion and remind us of the beginning by relating to it in a different, creative way.

Reviewing Your Essay

Once your essay is written you will want to apply a rubric to check for errors that could detract from the structure and content. Do this by examining your essay for organisation, voice, word choice, sentence structure, syntax, transitions, writing conventions and creativity.

Ask yourself the following questions:

Organisation

1. Does my beginning make sense? Is it well focused and clear?
2. Does my beginning show that I have tried to analyse the topic in an unusual way?
3. Are my ideas, details and examples that form my support organised in a coherent and effective manner?
4. Do I have at least three points that back up my thesis statement?
5. Have I analysed each piece of support and provided examples for that support?
6. Is there a conclusion that ties the pieces of the essay together?

Voice

1. Does my paper have an original voice – namely mine?
2. Have I given credit to all the sources in my essay and ensured that I have not plagiarised? In other words, have I kept someone else's content and voice separate from mine?
3. Is there a tone that enhances the essay?

Word Choice

1. Is my diction good? Have I tried to find words that convey my thoughts in a clear, precise, creative manner that uses sensory details (smell, touch, taste, sight, and sound)?
2. Have I used a wide range of vocabulary?
3. Have I used literary terms in the analysis?
4. Have I used concise language, and tightened ideas wherever I can?

Sentence Structure and Syntax

1. Am I following the basic rules of syntax to create clear sentences?
2. Do my sentences flow smoothly from point to point?
3. Are the sentences arranged effectively into paragraphs?

Transitions

1. Do I have clear transitions that connect paragraphs?

Writing Conventions

1. Am I following the basic rules of grammar, punctuation, spelling, and capitalisation?
2. Am I writing in the active voice? In other words, is my subject doing the action, rather the action being done to the subject?

Creativity

1. Have I found a different and interesting way of analysing and organising my subject matter?
2. Have I used figures of speech or descriptions that use the senses (sight, touch, smell, feel, taste) to make my essay feel alive?

Avoiding the Passive Voice

One of the major pitfalls of writing is the use of the passive voice. The passive voice makes an essay appear dull and lifeless because your subject is not doing the action. The action is being done to your subject.

This creates several problems. First of all, the passive voice inverts the most natural order of sentences, subject–verb–object, and so it leads the reader away from the action. Check the example below.

> The feelings of Antoinette are clouded by Mr Rochester's despicable affair with the servant girl.

This sentence is in the passive voice. Note that this sentence is not in the past tense: passive voice has nothing to do with past tense. For argument's sake let us say that the main point we want to convey here is Mr Rochester's despicable behaviour. It takes us a relatively long time to focus our attention on Mr Rochester and his behaviour.

The way the sentence is constructed, Antoinette's clouded feelings are more important just because of their position in the sentence. But our subject is still Mr Rochester. He is the one who is clouding the feelings. We need to tighten this sentence, and get the helping verb 'are' out of the sentence. We need to put Mr Rochester in control of the action so that we have the active voice.

When you do this exercise, you will often find that you want to play with the diction. You do not have to keep the same words when you change an awkward sentence in the passive voice into the active voice. Check the example below.

Mr Rochester's despicable affair with the servant girl, Amelie, devastates Antoinette.

There is one easy way to avoid the passive voice and that is to avoid using the helping verb 'to be' with another verb. Once you have a situation where the verb 'to be' is piggy-backing on another verb, you are likely to have the passive voice.

There is another important reason to use the active voice in your writing. It keeps you better focused. When you read literature, your mind is like a camera. You record the film that you put into it. If you make sure that you put your subject centre stage and then follow him (or her) alone throughout the essay, you will not stray to other events or other characters.

Using the active voice forces the writer to relate other characters to the subject. It offers little opportunity to stray. As the cameraman following this character around, you are always well focused.

Note: once you have written that first paragraph, you need to go back and check it to make sure that it is in the simple present tense and that your subject is doing your action. Like a good film editor, you need to keep checking back to make sure that you are focused on the correct scene – namely, those your subject is in – for this movie you have created.

Going back to make periodic checks saves a lot of valuable time and prevents you from having to rewrite an entire essay that you have lost control of along the way.

Building Essays around Themes

In part two we looked at the themes of *Wide Sargasso Sea*. Essay questions will often ask about the themes of a novel. This section shows how you can turn the themes of the book into thesis statements that can be proved in various essays.

To do this, simply ask yourself a question: what does the novel say about family? How does love play a role in the characters' lives? How does jealousy affect the characters? Why is culture important to the novel? How does loyalty affect the characters?

Here are some examples of themes that have been turned into thesis statements which can form the basis of an essay.

Theme	Thesis Statement
The importance of family	A stable family provides a firm foundation for a happy, secure life.
Jealousy's destructive force	Jealousy is a destructive force that clouds all sense of reason.
The importance of loyalty	Loyalty inspires a sense of trust that allows freedom of expression.
How culture impacts on character	Culture shapes the way that a character views the world.
The curse of beauty	Beauty does not always bring happiness.

Build on your thesis statements by continuing to ask the questions how and why the information in your thesis statement affects characters in the novel. Here are examples of how to develop two of the thesis statements listed above.

'A stable family provides a firm foundation for a happy, secure life.'

Antoinette Cosway Mason, the main character in *Wide Sargasso Sea*, is a vivid example of what happens to a person who comes from an unstable family. Author Jean Rhys shows how Antoinette's insecure childhood fills her with self-doubt, causes her to question her own sanity, and leads her into a disastrous marriage.

Now you have three points to prove: Antoinette has an insecure childhood filled with self-doubt; she questions her own sanity; and her unstable background leads her into a disastrous marriage.

'Jealousy is a destructive force that clouds all sense of reason.'

Author Jean Rhys demonstrates jealousy's destructive force throughout the novel *Wide Sargasso Sea*. Antoinette Cosway Mason, the main character in the novel, realises how jealousy destroys her mother's life as well as their family's estate, Coulibri, yet Antoinette cannot avoid the irrational feeling of jealousy in her own marriage to Mr Rochester.

Once again you have three points to prove: jealousy destroys Antoinette's mother; their home; and Antoinette's marriage.

Alternative Ways to Create a Beginning

Visual learners often find it difficult to write a thesis statement because of the abstract thinking that is involved. One of the best ways to skirt this problem is to create an anecdote to anchor your essay. Usually, if you think of the scene that stands out most in your mind and try to condense what happens into a short paragraph, you will have the essence of the thesis statement embodied in that visual description.

An anecdote helps to focus attention on a smaller piece of information and allows readers, who might otherwise feel overwhelmed by the amount of information to analyse, a chance to concentrate on the most important point that stands out in your mind.

Here is an example of an anecdote and how it focuses a thesis statement:

'Get in the coach!' Mr Mason yelled frantically, and when Antoinette, sleepy and full of fear, turned towards the house from which her family had just fled, she witnessed a horrible sight. Coco, the parrot, whose wings had been clipped, sat on the rail, his feathers on fire. Antoinette could hear the angry crowd that had set her family's estate on fire, but she could not stop watching Coco.

The next step is to start asking those what, how, and why questions.
1. Why did this scene stand out in my mind?
2. How does this scene represent the themes of *Wide Sargasso Sea*?
3. What is going on in this scene?

The answer to one of these questions will be the focus of that transition which will lead us into the analysis of the novel. This transition functions almost like a thesis statement.

Here is an example of a direction in which you can take your writing after you have established an anecdote:

The sad scene of Antoinette witnessing the death of the family parrot represents, in many ways, the loss of innocence (or security). With her home burning and her pet parrot dying, Antoinette must realise that there is no safe place in this world.

The task now is to prove that this anecdote shows either the loss of innocence or the loss of security. As you develop your essay, you have this snapshot of the novel to constantly anchor your thoughts.

Using Figures of Speech

Sometimes a metaphor or a simile can be an effective way of anchoring your thoughts. Figures of speech can be haunting reminders of a visual image that leads to or develops a theme. It is impossible to watch the movie *Forrest Gump* and not think of starting an essay with 'Life is like a box of chocolates. You never know what you're going to get.'

Think of some themes from *Wide Sargasso Sea* and try to turn them into similes.

Here is the process:
1. Find the theme by asking yourself: what is the essence of the novel?

2. Turn the theme into a simile by relating the theme you are going to analyse to an object.
3. Explain what your simile means.
4. Find an example from the book to back up your analysis of the simile.
5. Keep relating your information back to your simile.

Here is an example:

> Jealousy is like a balloon that bursts. Initially, there is the carefree feeling of floating aimlessly in the sky, but when an unforeseen force makes that balloon explode, there is no way to recover the original feeling of euphoria.

The Funnel

Some students need to establish the big picture before they can analyse the pieces of the puzzle. They see a broad general scope for an essay and then they break that down into specific pieces.

This too is an effective way of writing, provided that you keep in mind that it is necessary to move from general ideas to specific ideas as quickly as possible. Remember, once you have established your general point and move on to how it specifically relates to the novel, you cannot go back to the general point again. You must keep developing your specific points until you reach the conclusion of the essay.

The information in this essay really should look like a funnel, broad at the top and narrow at the bottom.

Sample Essay using the Funnel

Here is an example of an essay that uses a funnel and answers the question 'Why does Annette Mason go mad?'

> Any sane person can go mad once there are forces or circumstances that completely obliterate a person's sense of self. Annette Cosway, Antoinette's beautiful mother, is certainly a victim of such circumstances.

Annette has a litany of woes that cause undue stress in her life. There are neighbours who hate and threaten her, and a husband who dismisses her fears. He does not heed her observations about the danger that threatens the family and the financial problems that make independence impossible.

Antoinette's mother, Annette Cosway, is hard pressed to find a friend she can confide in, because no one seems to like her. Those who do not, exclude her because they are jealous of her beauty, or ignore her because she is unlike everyone else. She is scorned because she is considered white. Black Jamaicans had recently been emancipated, and they were busy venting their anger and frustration against white people who reminded them of their days in bondage. Jamaicans also look down on Annette because she is from Martinique, a French island that the Jamaicans considered to be backward and full of superstition and evil practices such as obeah.

Totally isolated in a foreign land where she is hated, Annette slips into depression and madness. It does not seem that she has much choice. She is unable to salvage any piece of her identity. Her beauty, nationality, race, and her very presence in a foreign country form a threat to the Jamaicans who harass her. As the walls close in she retreats deeper inside herself.

Annette Cosway makes one desperate attempt to save herself: she marries Mr Mason. This must have been an extraordinary effort because by the time she meets Mr Mason, her trust is basically gone. Any love Annette has for her new, ambitious husband who is determined to save her home, Coulibri Estate, is dashed when she realises that she cannot confide in him. Her fears and warnings of imminent danger fall on deaf ears. Mr Mason does not fear Jamaicans, or life, as his wife does. This must seem like the ultimate betrayal for Annette.

Annette's problems are not confined to social or personal situations: financial problems also plague her. Before she marries Mr Mason, life is hard and Annette has to find ways to keep her estate running when none of the newly freed slaves want to work on the plantations again. Life seems to improve financially when Mr Mason arrives, but when fire destroys Coulibri Estate, Annette is left with nothing. Money worries can be the most debilitating problem anyone has to face in life. Annette has enough money worries to send her over the edge.

If Annette Cosway Mason could have found one thin thread of hope to hang on to, she might not have gone insane. Unfortunately, everywhere she turned she met cruelty, danger, and callousness. The only way to survive physically was to retreat into the shell that we call madness.

Analysing the Funnel Essay 'Why does Annette Mason Go Mad?'

1. The first sentence in the essay contains the funnel statement, a general statement that sets the boundaries for the essay. Note that the end of the first sentence focuses our attention on what kind of information you are looking for: examples of circumstances that would obliterate someone's sense of self.
2. The second sentence focuses on specific information and tells us which character we are going to examine, to make that general point about how sane people can go insane.
3. Specific points that are going to be used for proof are now listed. This is not a typical format for an essay, but it is used here to show how you can vary structure.
4. The support of the essay follows. Each one of the listed points is analysed. There are two paragraphs for the first point and one paragraph for the other two points.
5. Finally, there is a conclusion that ties all the pieces together.

Further Sample Essays

Persuasive Essays

Persuasive essays require the writer to relate to a question by taking a stand for or against. Here is a question that could be used for a persuasive essay. Notice how the sentences are constructed so that Antoinette is always the focus. It would be easy to switch to Mr Rochester's point of view and make him the focus of the sentence, but this could result in losing control of the sentence.

'Is there any way that Antoinette could have prevented Mr Rochester from losing interest in her?'

Antoinette, the Creole girl who marries Mr Rochester in the novel *Wide Sargasso Sea*, never stands a chance of keeping her husband. Her marriage is doomed from the beginning. The main problem is the fact that Antoinette has virtually an arranged marriage. Besides this, she lacks the psychological and cultural knowledge of how to deal with an English husband.

Antoinette would have stood a better chance with her husband if he had met her on his own and not through the arrangements of his family and hers. She finds herself the object of Mr Rochester's scorn because he feels forced into the marriage so that his father does not have to divide his property. It is difficult for Antoinette to cultivate any sense of love with a man who resents her because he did not get to know her and make his own choice to marry her.

After the marriage Antoinette has to struggle to make a marriage work that was doomed from the beginning. She finds her husband becoming more and more irritable and restless because he doubts his decision to marry her. She does not know that these feelings come from the pressures he felt from his father, and the anger and fear of embarrassment he experienced when Antoinette tried to call off the marriage. Antoinette feels tremendous psychological pressure to please her reticent husband, who is not communicating his feelings to her. She does not realise that his behaviour, which includes a cruel and meaningless affair with her servant Amelie, is his vain attempt to punish those around him for his feelings of being trapped.

The marriage is also hindered by both parties' inability to understand each other's culture. Antoinette has no idea of how a proper Englishwoman behaves and so her loyalty to her servants, leisurely attitude towards chores, and emotional outbursts seem strange and out of place to Mr Rochester. Their ideas of loyalty are also determined by culture. Antoinette's loyalty to Christophene irritates Mr Rochester. Antoinette respects Christophene's advice because Christophene has been loyal since Antoinette was a child. She does not understand Mr Rochester's distrust of her, which stems partly from Daniel Cosway's warnings about her practising obeah. Antoinette and her husband often seem to be operating in two different worlds, with no way to bridge the gap between their cultural differences.

There is no doubt that Antoinette is overburdened with the emotional stress of a marriage that Mr Rochester feels was forced upon him. This burden is compounded by the fact that neither Antoinette nor Mr Rochester understands the other's emotion or culture. There is little opportunity for Antoinette to construct a happy ending out of such an unhappy beginning, based on too much manipulation and too many misunderstandings.

Analysing the Persuasive Essay

The assignment above, 'Is there any way that Antoinette could have prevented Mr Rochester from losing interest in her?', requires a persuasive essay. The writer has to take a stand and support that viewpoint with specific literary evidence from the novel. Here, we have two choices: either there was a way for Antoinette to control her marriage, or there was no way that she could have kept her husband from losing interest in her.

A good persuasive essay requires firm control over the subject matter. The writer has to choose a structure that helps to focus the information. This essay follows events in the marriage in chronological order. The essay begins with some analysis before the marriage. Note that Antoinette's struggle to maintain control is the focus in each sentence.

It would be easy to slip off into Mr Rochester's point of view and try to relate his plight back to Antoinette, but this could cause the essay structure to meander. It is better to keep Antoinette the focus of the essay by constructing sentences that are about her. Think of an essay as a camera keeping the subject in view. You need to keep Antoinette in focus, just as you would make her the subject of a picture.

Controlling an essay that deals with the problems of a specific character generally boils down to relating everything back to that one character named in the essay question.

Paragraph One

The first paragraph directly states the viewpoint of the essay. Since the purpose of the assignment is to write a persuasive essay, it is best to be direct and get to the point from the very beginning of the essay. The three points that will be examined in this essay are included in the opening paragraph with the thesis statement.

Paragraphs Two, Three and Four

Each paragraph takes one piece of support laid out in the thesis statement and develops arguments for that support. Paragraph one deals with the problems of having an arranged marriage. Paragraph two analyses the psychological problems associated with the marriage and paragraph three examines the cultural problems. Specific examples are provided for each point.

Paragraph Five

The conclusion loops back to the beginning, but does not merely restate the beginning. The conclusion adds more details than the beginning and reminds the reader what the whole essay was about.

Essays using Figures of Speech

'Caught in the Wide Sargasso Sea'

Trapped in a tangled web of intrigue and deception: that's the fate of most of the characters in Jean Rhys's novel *Wide Sargasso Sea*. Caught in the past and tangled in their own sense of culture, Antoinette, her mother, Annette, and Mr Rochester thrash about with nowhere to go and nowhere to hide.

Like the slowly circling pool of algae-ridden water known as the Sargasso Sea which sits between Europe and the West Indies, Antoinette and her husband, Mr Rochester, float aimlessly, unable to escape the confinement of their new marriage. Neither character is able to move beyond the sea of despair that they create for one another. Mr Rochester suffers from bouts of nostalgia for England, while Antoinette suffers from insecurity.

Mr Rochester finds the West Indies backward and stagnant with prejudice; he hates it. He feels trapped by his father's plan to marry him to Antoinette so that his father would not have to divide his precious land. He feels trapped because Richard Mason, Antoinette's brother, does not divulge the family's history of mental illness. He feels trapped by Antoinette's beauty, which he finds is nothing more than a cover for the madness that lies beneath.

Trapped in her own sea of despair, Antoinette grows up isolated from the Jamaican culture that has deemed her a 'white cockroach'. Her life must seem like a lonely boat trapped in the Sargasso Sea – she does not even have the comfort of her mother. Frightened that there is no escape from her past or the madness that consumed her mother, Antoinette struggles to free herself from her own Sargasso Sea before she marries Mr Rochester: she tries in vain to call off the wedding. But, consumed by jealousy and the fear of embarrassment, Mr Rochester allows Antoinette no way out of the pending marriage.

No character stands alone in *Wide Sargasso Sea*. The tangled web of despair that ties everyone together reflects the tangled web in which countless innocent people have perished in the Sargasso Sea.

One of those innocent victims is Antoinette's mother, Annette, who can find no escape from the prejudice and fear that she feels in Spanish Town. She cannot cross her sea of despair and return to Martinique where she was born, and she is resented in Jamaica because she is from the French island. Annette sees no way out of her troubled life and she is finally destroyed when restless, angry natives raze her home, Coulibri Estate. She thrashes about emotionally for some time, but she is not able to live with the death of her invalid son, Pierre, after the fire, or with the feeling that she has been betrayed by her own husband, Mr Mason, because he always dismisses her fears as irrational.

The wide Sargasso Sea consumes Antoinette and her family and, although in the end she reaches England with her husband, both characters remain emotionally lost in the stagnant sea that separates their two lands.

Analysing the Essay using Figures of Speech

This essay shows the significance of the novel's title. Here we investigate the writing process.

Opening paragraph

The wide Sargasso Sea serves as a visual symbol that links together the characters in Jean Rhys's novel of the same name. The essay above looks at the characters' tangled lives and relates that metaphorically to the Sargasso Sea in the Atlantic Ocean. The essay begins with an analysis of that tangled web, made up of lies and deception.

That web could include nearly every character in the novel, but in order to stay focused, this essay clearly states that we will be looking at three people: Antoinette, her mother, and her husband. This allows us to remain on track in an essay that could become unwieldy by including too many characters.

Second Paragraph – The Introduction to Support

By the second paragraph, the characters are linked to the seaweed of the Sargasso Sea that lends its name to the novel. We begin to concentrate on Mr Rochester and Antoinette as a couple. Then we break them up as individuals in the next two paragraphs to make the analysis simpler.

Third and Fourth Paragraphs – The Heart of our Support

The third paragraph concentrates on Mr Rochester while the fourth concentrates on Antoinette.

Fifth Paragraph – a Transition

Any good essay should have at least three points that prove the thesis statement. Antoinette's mother makes up our third example of support. There's one small problem: she has not been mentioned since the opening paragraph. We need a transition to tie her in with Antoinette and her husband, who form our main evidence. To throw her into the essay right after the preceding paragraphs with Antoinette and Mr Rochester might seem rather disconcerting. For this reason, the fifth paragraph serves as a transition.

The Sixth Paragraph – Additional Support

Now we are ready to tie in Antoinette's mother to the essay. We have set the essay up in a manner where our main support is on the top. This additional support proves that we are able to dig deeper into the novel and analyse characters other than the obvious ones.

After this paragraph we could add additional paragraphs analysing other characters. The structure is tight enough to accommodate other characters if there is enough time to write.

Note how the imagery of the sea weaves its way through the essay. This allows the reader to visualise some complicated abstract information. It also helps to create transitions and build a conclusion at the end of the essay.

The Conclusion

The conclusion ties together all the pieces. It makes a loop back to the beginning and reminds us of our imagery: the Sargasso Sea.

Part IV Study Questions, Essays and Assignments

In this part you will find some questions that will help you with your study of the novel and give you more essay-writing practice.

Study Questions

1. What symbolic significance can you attribute to Thornfield, the name of Mr Rochester's estate?
2. Describe Mr Rochester. Use the five methods of characterisation.
3. Do you think that Mr Rochester is an honourable person? What literary evidence do you have for your answer?
4. Is Mr Rochester honest? Give literary reasons to support your answer.
5. Antoinette Rochester is clearly portrayed as mad in *Jane Eyre*. How else is she portrayed?

Further Study Questions

Most of the following questions have no wrong or right answer. Use literary evidence from the novel *Wide Sargasso Sea* to make your own case.

1. What are some possible ways that Antoinette's family could have dealt with the prejudice that surrounded them?
2. What could Antoinette have done to prevent Mr Rochester from losing interest in her?
3. Is Christophene a help or a hindrance to Antoinette? Explain.
4. Does Richard Mason care about Antoinette? Explain.
5. How do culture and cultural differences play an important role in *Wide Sargasso Sea*?
6. Why does Daniel Cosway write letters to Mr Rochester? What does he achieve by writing these letters?

7. Why does Mr Rochester call Antoinette by the name of Bertha?
8. Many events in *Wide Sargasso Sea* seem to be self-fulfilling prophecies. Explain some of these events.
9. Why did Mr Rochester marry Antoinette?
10. What role does jealousy play in *Wide Sargasso Sea*?

Analysing Prose Passages

Analyse the following statements with a well-written paragraph that uses complete sentences.

1. Mr Luttrell seems to understand the position of the angry Jamaicans whom Annette Cosway Mason fears. He says: 'Of course they have their own misfortunes. Still waiting for this compensation the English promised when the Emancipation Act was passed.'
   'How could she know that Mr Luttrell would be the first who grew tired of waiting? One calm evening he shot his dog, swam out to sea and was gone for always' (p. 5).

2. When Antoinette's family is leaving their burning estate, their path is blocked. Aunt Cora steps forward and says that Pierre is hurt and that he will die if they do not get help for him.
   The man's reply is: 'So, black and white, they burn the same, eh?'
   'They do', says Aunt Cora. 'Here and hereafter, as you will find out. Very shortly' (p. 23).

3. Some time after the fire at Coulibri, Antoinette wakes up from her illness and asks about her younger brother. Her Aunt Cora replies, 'He died on the way down, the poor little boy.'
   'He died before that', Antoinette thinks.

4. When Mr Rochester questions Antoinette about her mother, he says: 'why did you tell me that she died when you were a child?'
   Antoinette replies: 'Because they told me to say so and because it is true. She did die when I was a child. There are always two deaths, the real one and the one people know about.' What does Antoinette mean by this statement?

5. Mr Rochester insists on calling Antoinette by the name of Bertha even though he knows it upsets her. What does Antoinette's reaction mean when she says: 'Bertha is not my name. You are trying to make me into someone else, calling me by another name. I know, that's obeah too.'

Suggested Essays

1. Although Annette and Antoinette are portrayed as sensitive, weak women, there are also examples of strong women in *Wide Sargasso Sea*. Write an essay examining the strong women in the novel.

   Your essay should include Aunt Cora, Christophene, and Amelie. What qualities do they possess which would categorise them as strong women? Important qualities here are their sense of independence and their ability to speak their mind.

2. Write an essay discussing the narrative voice in *Wide Sargasso Sea*.

   Your pre-writing work will require that you examine the following information.
   A. Who are the narrators in the novel?
      Part one: narrated by Antoinette
      Part two: narrated by Mr Rochester
      Part three: narrated by Grace Poole and Antoinette
   B. Would the novel have been better if it were narrated by Antoinette alone? Why or why not?

3. Why does Mr Rochester prefer Jane Eyre to Antoinette?
   This essay will only be possible if you have read *Jane Eyre*. Make a chart that analyses the personality traits of both women. Because of the way the question is worded, you will have to look at the two women through Mr Rochester's eyes.

4. Compare Antoinette to her mother.
   Consider the following:
   A. How are Antoinette and her mother alike? How are they different?
   B. Was Antoinette doomed to the same fate as her mother or were the circumstances that drove Antoinette mad different from those of her mother?

5. Setting plays an important role in a novel. Analyse the settings in *Wide Sargasso Sea* and write an essay about how they set a tone or mood.
   Make sure that you include the following settings:
   Coulibri Estate; Granbois Estate; Thornfield
   A. Examine what the settings have in common and what makes them different.
   B. What descriptions does Rhys use to convey the tone or mood of each setting?

6. Sometimes a minor character plays an important role in a novel. Choose a minor character and write an essay about how that character plays a pivotal role in the story.
   Note: in an essay such as this, you must be careful that there is enough information to prove that your character has a major impact, even though he or she is only a minor character.
   You need to be able to explain what role the character plays and make sure that you can come up with at least three incidents that can be used for support. It is important that you do this in the pre-writing stage, or you will find yourself with an essay that is too short and too shallow.
   Which of the following characters would be sufficient to build your argument? Jot down information on each character to determine which ones have enough information to build your case.
   1. Daniel Cosway
   2. Pierre Cosway
   3. Amelie
   4. Mr Luttrell
   5. Aunt Cora
   6. Grace Poole
   7. Richard Mason

7. Prejudice is a major theme in *Wide Sargasso Sea*. Write an essay discussing the many faces of prejudice in the novel.
   For this essay you need to examine the following:
   A. Racial prejudice – ex-slaves against the white Creoles.
   B. Social prejudice – Daniel Cosway's feelings about Antoinette.

C. Cultural prejudice –
   1. Mr Rochester's cultural prejudices, including his feelings about Christophene.
   2. His feelings about his wife.

8. Several animals create powerful symbols in *Wide Sargasso Sea*. Write an essay discussing these animals and what they symbolise. Your essay should include the following:
   A. Annette Cosway's poisoned horse.
   B. The parrot who burned at Coulibri Estate.
   C. The term 'white cockroach' that is used to describe Antoinette.
   D. Mr Luttrell's dog that was shot before he committed suicide.

9. What role does jealousy play in the novel?
   Your essay needs to examine the following points:
   A. The freed slaves' jealousy of the status and money that they perceive the white Creoles to have.
   B. The white Creoles' jealousy of Annette Cosway Mason's beauty.
   C. Mr Rochester's jealousy when he hears rumours of Antoinette's relationship with other men, specifically Sandi Cosway.
   D. Antoinette's jealousy when she perceives Mr Rochester is flirting with Amelie and her outrage when she finds out he had an affair with her.
   E. Daniel Cosway's jealousy over Antoinette's social status and the bitter letters he writes to Mr Rochester because of it.
   F. Mr Rochester's jealousy over his wife's loyalty to Christophene.

   This essay has the possibility of at least six points for support. Your challenge now is to organise these points into an essay by using the process below.
   1. First consider any other possibilities of jealousy in the novel. Are there any other references to jealousy that you could use in the essay?
   2. Look at the six points above and try to determine categories that would allow you to group any of these points together.
   You will note that A, B, and E all have to do with jealousy that

results from social status while C, D and F have to do with jealousy that stems from love, infatuation and possessiveness.

You have now organised your points into a tighter structure. Instead of developing six different points, you have the possibility of developing two major points with three pieces of support for each point.

10. Throughout *Jane Eyre* and *Wide Sargasso Sea*, Mr Rochester claims that he married Antoinette because he was tricked by her family and his. What other reasons does Mr Rochester have for marrying Antoinette?

Although there is a fair amount of information that is used to set up this question, the question is really quite straightforward and simple. All the question requires the writer to do is to probe deeper into Mr Rochester's motives for marriage.

Since the question requires you to find other reasons for his marriage, you will have to begin by investigating your subject's motives. Do this by searching for evidence in the book.

A. If he has doubts about the wedding – and Mr Rochester expresses many such doubts – why does he go through with the wedding when Antoinette wants to back out?

B. What initially attracts Mr Rochester to Antoinette?

C. What does Mr Rochester stand to gain from the marriage?

11. Write a character analysis of Christophene.

A. Make sure that you use the five methods of characterisation.

B. Identify Christophene as a stock or dynamic character.

C. Use sensory details:

Christophene is a colourful character, who lends herself very well to most of the five senses. Within your analysis describes how she looks, smells, sounds, and feels.

Christophene is described as an obeah woman so you should be able to conjure up a dark, mysterious picture of her in words. Imagine how she smells from scenes in the book. How does she sound when she talks? Imagine Antoinette trying to hug her as a child. How would she feel?

Note: if you have a difficult time conjuring up images of characters, try drawing a picture using descriptions and information from the text.

12. Write an essay analysing Daniel Cosway's letter.
    Ask the following questions before you start writing your essay.
    A. What does Daniel Cosway hope to achieve by writing the letter?
    B. What is the tone of the letter?
    C. What purpose does the letter serve in the book?
       a. What important information does it provide about the characters?
       b. What conflicts does it create?
       c. How does it help to advance the plot?
       d. How would the book have been different without the letter?

Further Suggested Assignments

1. Choose a character, Mr Rochester or Antoinette, and prepare a role play that will answer the accusations in Daniel Cosway's letters.
2. Write a news story about the night that Coulibri Estate was burned down. Make sure you have a gripping lead that answers the questions who, what, when, where and why.
3. What help could Antoinette get now if she were suffering from mental illness? Do research about the psychological and medical treatment available for mental illness today. Include information from the Internet, interviews with doctors and social services.
4. You are answering the advert to take care of Antoinette. What questions would you ask about your job? Prepare questions to ask your employer. What demands would you make for salary and working conditions?
5. Pretend Mr Rochester is on trial for cruel and unusual punishment towards Antoinette. Appoint a judge, jury, a defence lawyer and someone to make the prosecution's case. You must use information from *Jane Eyre* and *Wide Sargasso Sea* to make your case.

6. Use the descriptions in *Wide Sargasso Sea* to draw a picture of Coulibri Estate.

7. Draw a portrait of Antoinette using descriptions from the novel.

8. Pretend you are an advice columnist giving tips to Antoinette. Write a letter as if from Antoinette, about her marital problems. Then answer the questions as an advice columnist would in a newspaper.

9. Neither *Wide Sargasso Sea* nor *Jane Eyre* covers Antoinette's voyage between the West Indies and England. Pretend you are Antoinette and keep a diary of that voyage. What are you feeling as you make that transition?

10. Is madness hereditary or is it determined by the environment? Can it be a combination of both? Look up information on the Internet and prepare a poster board that gives information about mental health.

Answers

Answers to Vocabulary Exercise

1. vulnerable
2. capricious
3. posthumously
4. disconcerting
5. disdainful
6. sully or debase
7. obstinate
8. bane
9. impeccable
10. abominable

Answers to *Wide Sargasso Sea* Quiz

1. Christophene says the 'white' people are jealous of Annette because she is pretty and because she is from Martinique. This shows that they are petty and prejudiced. They feel that Annette is inferior because she is from one of the small islands.
2. When the doctor examines Pierre Cosway he tells Annette that nothing can be done to help him. This appears to be the last straw for her. She becomes thin and reclusive. Basically, she gives up on life. There seems to be no hope left when she has to accept the news about her son.
3. Like the Garden of Eden, Coulibri offers hope and serenity in paradise, but all of this vanishes because of the evil that invades the paradise. In this case it is the repercussions of the evil of slavery.
4. Christophene loses any possibility of status among the former slaves because she is loyal to a white family. She is categorised as a traitor. Everyone regards Christophene with suspicion even before this, because she is from one of the small islands and it is rumoured that she practises obeah.

5. The children call Antoinette a white cockroach. A cockroach is a vile bug that is hated by everyone. It is ugly and dirty. The children seem to want to ensure that this ugly, dirty image is attached to her race and so they qualify the description by calling her a white cockroach.

6. It is rumoured that emancipation trouble killed old Cosway, but most people attribute his death to his drinking. Some also say that he was mad.

7. Those who gossip about Annette Cosway's marriage to Mr Mason make it clear that he has money. Although no one offers a clear explanation of why he married her, he seems to have been in love with her – she has little to offer emotionally or even financially. Perhaps Mr Mason was charmed by Annette's beauty or the challenge of rescuing her as well as her dilapidated estate.

8. Mr Mason does not like Aunt Cora because he feels that she got away from the trouble and prejudice that other former slave owners were still paying for. He does not seem to feel that there is a sense of justice in this.

9. Mr Mason is a kind, generous man who is somewhat naive. He marries Annette in spite of the fact that public opinion is against her. He repairs Coulibri and he is kind to Annette's children. He is somewhat naive, however, because he does not see how angry and restless the newly freed black slaves are. He doubts Annette's fears and dismisses the blacks as lazy but not dangerous.

10. Antoinette says that it is very unlucky to kill a parrot, so the parrot serves the symbolic purpose of foreshadowing the bad luck that haunts Antoinette in the future. The parrot also symbolises the loss of paradise as it once must have been in Coulibri. Along the way everything went wrong and Antoinette's family are like the parrot, once free and later confined to the estate as though their wings had been clipped.

11. During the fire that consumed Coulibri Estate Annette fights her husband, Mr Mason, to return to the burning house to save Coco the parrot. Aunt Cora advises her to stop fighting. She tells Annette that the people who set the fire are looking at her.

Although Aunt Cora does not say it, her advice is that Annette should keep her dignity in front of the people who have caused her to suffer. Dignity, after all, is all that the family has left.

12. Antoinette's mother goes mad and she is kept by people in a house in the country. She eventually dies. Antoinette does not know the details because she is not even told of her mother's death.

13. The village name of Massacre adds verbal irony to the story. It is ironic that the village name is Massacre but no one remembers why. Hope is massacred here. The shaky marriage falls apart in everything but name only, and Antoinette's emotions are certainty slaughtered by Mr Rochester's indiscretions.

14. Antoinette is never able to feel safe and secure after the fire at Coulibri. That insecurity makes it impossible for her fully to love or trust anyone.

15. Daniel Cosway shows anger and jealousy in the letter. He is jealous because Antoinette had a social position that he never had because he was illegitimate. His anger is reflected in his description of the Cosways as 'wicked and detestable'.

16. Antoinette is clearly disturbed by Mr Rochester's decision to call her Bertha. It is not her name, and so she thinks he does it to irritate her. Also, she tells Christophene that he has found out that it was her mother's name. This puts Antoinette in an uncomfortable position because Mr Rochester is virtually saying she is like her mother: crazy.

17. Daniel Cosway says that Christophene had to leave Spanish Town because she was accused of practising obeah and she was imprisoned for it. Mr Rochester writes to the lawyer, Mr Fraser, enquiring about Christophene, and finds out that she was imprisoned. He does not give details about the charge, but says that he found her to be a shady character.

18. There are many possible explanations about why Mr Rochester takes Antoinette to England with him. His decision seems to be based in part on his sense of duty to his father, but it is also based on his need to feel that he is in control of the situation and that he is not abandoning his responsibilities.

It is also possible that he does not want Christophene to have the satisfaction of providing a new life for Antoinette. Mr Rochester and Christophene had a bitter quarrel before he dismissed her. She accused him of wanting Antoinette's money and she suggested that Mr Rochester return half of the dowry and allow Antoinette to pursue her own life in Martinique. Mr Rochester was outraged. He would never agree to this. He would never give Christophene the satisfaction of feeling that she had won out over him.

19. In part three of *Wide Sargasso Sea*, Antoinette is locked away in the tower because she is supposedly mad. She says that she does not believe she is in England. Her emotional state obviously caused her to be disoriented on the trip across the ocean. Still, she is sane enough to tell her story and let us know that people say she is in England. Sadly, Antoinette does not believe she is in England because it is not as she dreamed it would be.

20. With nothing more than a flickering candle to light her way, Antoinette walks through the dark passage of Thornfield, which is much like the dark journey across the ocean that slaves took in what is known as the Middle Passage.

Answers to Study Questions

1. Metaphorically speaking, the name of Mr Rochester's estate, Thornfield, stands for the pain, emotional and physical, that both Antoinette and Jane feel. Relatively isolated, Thornfield is a lonely, drab, and painful place; it is Antoinette's prison. Thornfield also symbolises Jane Eyre's thorny relationship with Mr Rochester.

2. Mr Rochester is twenty years older than Jane. At thirty-eight, he seems unsettled, sad and sometimes bitter. He is secretive and he shows signs of kindness with Jane and Adele, the child of a former lover whom he brings to Thornfield. He can be cruel and deceptive. His actions sometimes upset Jane. He hides Antoinette from her. Most of the characters in the novel seem to have a high opinion of Mr Rochester. They speak of him fondly

and protectively. He thinks highly of Jane, but he is troubled by his past.

3. There are many possible answers for this question. It all depends on how you decide to interpret the information. You will have to answer some of the following questions to come up with your answer. When Mr Rochester brings Antoinette to England, does he provide a home for her or a prison? When he does not tell Jane about Antoinette, is he protecting Jane or hiding something from her? Can you justify his attempt at bigamy? Do his intentions towards Jane seem honourable? Do his relationships with other people suggest that he is honourable? Consider his servants and Miss Ingram.

4. Mr Rochester often appears to be dishonest. He hides Antoinette from Jane and he even tries to commit bigamy.

5. Antoinette is also portrayed as evil and vindictive. She tries to kill Mr Rochester. She is described as a vampire.

Answers to Further Study Questions

1. Prejudice is difficult to counteract because it is an opinion based on emotion and misinformation rather than logic and facts. Still, there are some points to consider when determining whether or not Antoinette's family could have alleviated prejudice.
    A. Was their family's isolation enforced by events or did their family's isolation encourage prejudice?
    B. Did the family do everything it could do to involve the community in their estate? Did they offer jobs? Were they in any position to contribute in other ways to the community?

2. The answer to this question depends on whether or not you feel that anything else could have been said or done to save this troubled relationship.
    A. Did Antoinette communicate effectively with Mr Rochester?
    B. Was she too suspicious?
    C. Could she have helped him to adjust to the culture in any way?

D. Was she in an emotional state that was conducive to effective communication?

3. The best way to tackle this question is to weigh Christophene's words to both Antoinette and Mr Rochester. Make a list of how Christophene's advice seems helpful or not. Take quotations and put them under the two categories. You will soon get a picture.

4. Approach this question in the same way that you approach question three. Search for passages that include what Richard Mason says to Antoinette and Mr Rochester. Divide them up on a sheet of paper, with one column expressing the pros and the other expressing the cons. Make sure that you also include statements that other people make about Richard Mason. What other people say about a character carries a great deal of value in literature.

5. Culture plays an important role in how people think and how they relate to each other. You could approach this question by discussing or making a list of the cultural differences between the West Indies and England. You will have to put those differences into perspective historically speaking, but you could also look at some of the differences today to get an idea of what it would have been like back then. Ask yourself the following questions:

    A How did England feel about the West Indies at the time? Was it considered to be a developed area or a colony? What has changed today, if anything, in the way that England views the West Indies?

    B. What rights did women have in England in the 1830s?

    C. Did Caribbean women have the same rights as English women?

    D. Mr Rochester knows both England and the Caribbean while Antoinette knows only the Caribbean. Would that have made a difference in their relationship?

    E. What customs were associated with marriage in those days in England and the Caribbean? Were marriages arranged in both cultures? We know that women were not imported from the Caribbean to marry in England, but did people in the Caribbean send for people in England to marry in the colonies?

6. Scrutinise Daniel Cosway's letter and separate fact from emotion. What emotions does Daniel Cosway express? This will offer a key as to why he is writing these letters to Mr Rochester.

7. Antoinette is quite upset when Mr Rochester calls her Bertha. She tells him: 'Don't call me that. It's not my name.' He replies: 'I like that name.' Why do people call others by names that do not belong to them? As yourself the following questions:
   A. Is there any malice on Mr Rochester's part when he calls Antoinette by the name of Bertha?
   B. Does he show any affection when he calls her by this name?
   C. Often names carry a feeling associated with their sound. What kind of name is Bertha? Does it carry a sweet, melodious sound or a heavy, discordant sound?
   D. Does Mr Rochester stop calling Antoinette Bertha when she protests about the name?

8. There are at least three points to ponder in order to answer the question of whether or not certain events are self-fulfilling prophecies in *Wide Sargasso Sea*. In order to answer this question, we have to consider whether or not events could have been avoided if people had behaved differently. Are we a victim of circumstances or do we, as individuals, create circumstances in our lives? Look at the following three events.
   A. Annette, Antoinette's mother, constantly predicts disaster for her family and Coulibri Estate. It is finally burned down by angry Jamaicans. Do her dire predictions result from her own actions in any way?
   B. Antoinette constantly accuses Mr Rochester of siding with Amelie. Do Antoinette's jealousy and her constant accusations push Mr Rochester towards Amelie?
   C. Antoinette constantly fears that she will go insane like her mother. Does her constant worrying create circumstances that are conducive to her going insane?

9. Mr Rochester constantly argues that he was duped into his marriage with Antoinette. Do you accept this answer?

Consider the following questions:

A. What reasons does he have to marry Antoinette?

B. What was his relationship with his father?

C. What was his mental state before he became ill?

D. Does Mr Rochester express any feelings for Antoinette before or after the marriage?

E. Is he physically attracted to her and, if so, how would this have affected his decision to marry her?

F. What is his financial state before and after marrying Antoinette?

G. What is his reaction to certain circumstances, such as Richard Mason's announcement that Antoinette has decided to back out of the marriage at the last minute?

H. What emotions can contribute to someone's decision to marry or not?

10. Jealousy appears to be a powerful emotion in *Wide Sargasso Sea*. What role does jealousy play for the following characters?

1. Antoinette – Antoinette guards her new husband Mr Rochester with a fierce sense of jealousy.

2. Mr Rochester – Although he has no use for Antoinette, Mr Rochester admits to pangs of jealousy when certain people in the novel describe her as a beautiful girl, who was sought after by other men.

3. Daniel Cosway – Daniel Cosway deliberately sets out to destroy any possibility of happiness that Antoinette might have in her new marriage because he is jealous of her status in life. Because he is an illegitimate child with no social connections to the Cosway family, he decided that he will destroy her.

4. Amelie – flirts shamelessly with Mr Rochester. She too appears to be jealous of Antoinette's status. Amelie feels no remorse for her inappropriate behaviour because she has no feelings for Antoinette, and there is no reason other than jealousy for Amelie to dislike Antoinette.

Clearly, jealousy results from the frightening, empty feeling that comes from losing one's sense of power. Whenever one of the characters feels that his or her sense of power is being threatened, the character reacts jealously.

Answers to Analysing Prose Passages

1. Jean Rhys connects the restlessness of the newly freed slaves to the restlessness of the former slave owners who are living in fear, by playing on the word 'waiting'. The former slaves are growing tired of waiting for compensation the British promised before the Emancipation Act. Mr Luttrell apparently grows tired of waiting for a solution to the tension and so he kills himself.

2. Aunt Cora's remarks respond to the man who says, 'black and white, they burn the same'. This shows that she feels all people have to pay for their sins on earth, perhaps through the law. In death, those who do wrong will burn in hell. Punishment for wrongdoing on this earth and in the afterlife has nothing to do with colour.

3. Although Pierre dies from the burns that he sustains in the fire at Coulibri, Antoinette feels that, emotionally speaking, he really died before that. His physical and mental handicaps meant that he did not really exist because he was not able to participate in life on any kind of meaningful level.

4. Antoinette's statement about her mother's death means that she believes there are two types of death: the emotional one that is suffered in silence and the physical one that is visible to everyone else.

5. Antoinette believes that her husband's insistence on calling her by a name other than her own is like obeah because both work on the premise of destabilising a person and making them feel insecure. It is the ritualised action, in this case the name calling, that creates a sense of power in the person who applies it and confusion in the recipient of the action. The name, like obeah, relies heavily on symbolism. It associates Antoinette with her mother and her mother's mental state.

Selected Works of Jean Rhys

The Left Bank and Other Stories, 1927
Postures, 1928 (as *Quartet* in 1929); film, 1981
translator: *Perversity* (by Francis Carco), 1928
After Leaving Mr Mackenzie, 1931
translator: *Barred* (by Edward de Nève), 1932
Voyage in the Dark, 1934
Good Morning, Midnight, 1939; television film, 1959
Wide Sargasso Sea, 1966; film, 1992
Tigers Are Better-Looking, 1968
Penguin Modern Stories 1, 1969 (with others)
My Day: Three Pieces, 1975
Sleep It Off, Lady, 1976
Smile Please: An Unfinished Autobiography, 1979
Jean Rhys: Letters 1931–1966, 1984
Early Novels, 1984
The Complete Novels, 1985
Tales of the Wide Caribbean, 1985
The Collected Short Stories, 1987

Bibliography

1. Brontë, Charlotte, *Jane Eyre*, New York: Modern Library Paperback Edition, 2000
2. Rhys, Jean, *Wide Sargasso Sea*, London: Penguin, 1997
3. Smith, Angela, Introduction, *Wide Sargasso Sea*, London: Penguin, 1997
4. Wyndham, Francis and Melly, Diana, *Jean Rhys: Letters 1931–1966*, London: Andre Deutsch, 1984
5. National Library of Jamaica, 'A History of Spanish Town', 1997–2002
6. National Geographic (online), 'Sargasso Sea'